William M Clark

Sterling Dialogues

A choice collection of original dialogues suitable for day schools, Sunday schools,

lyceums, anniversaries, holidays, etc

William M Clark

Sterling Dialogues
A choice collection of original dialogues suitable for day schools, Sunday schools, lyceums, anniversaries, holidays, etc

ISBN/EAN: 9783337288570

Printed in Europe, USA, Canada, Australia, Japan

Cover: Foto ©Lupo / pixelio.de

More available books at **www.hansebooks.com**

STERLING DIALOGUES

A CHOICE COLLECTION OF ORIGINAL DIALOGUES SUITABLE FOR DAY-SCHOOLS, SUNDAY-SCHOOLS, LYCEUMS, ANNIVERSARIES, HOLIDAYS, ETC.

Compiled by
William M. Clark

PHILADELPHIA
THE PENN PUBLISHING COMPANY
1929

Copyright 1898, by The Penn Publishing Company

CONTENTS

		PAGE
OLD HEADS ON YOUNG SHOULDERS	Mrs. Louise E. V. Boyd	5
JUST FROM THE CITY	H. Elliott McBride	13
TRUSTY AND TRUE	Mrs. Clara A. Sylvester	20
UNAPPRECIATED GENIUS	Millie M. Olcott	28
THE DISCONTENTED GIRLS	Mrs. J. E. McConaughy	34
COLORADO—Acting Charade	Millie M. Olcott	35
A PAIR OF LIONS	Harry H. Cushing	37
THE CONJUGATING GERMAN	Vale Chester	48
WHERE THERE'S A WILL THERE'S A WAY—Dramatic Proverb	Sophie May	50
OTHER PEOPLE'S CHILDREN	Mrs. E. R. A.	58
GOOD MAXIMS		62
THE FLORAL GUIDE—A Tableau	Millie M. Olcott	63
THE THREE WISHES	Edward Traill Horn	64
TURN ABOUT'S FAIR PLAY	Hattie Herbert	67
FRIGHTENED AT NOTHING		74
BOARDING 'ROUND	Phila H. Case	78
ALICE'S PARTY	Eliza Doolittle	82
WHO'S THE POET?	Kate Woodland	86
I GUESS I'M THE MAN	Laura S. Parsons	90
MISCHIEF—Dramatic Charade	T. A. E. Holcomb	92
UNCLE DEAL'S LECTURE	Alice A. Coale	100
THE FAIRY QUEEN'S DECISION	Mrs. Louise E. V. Boyd	104
THE SECOND PRIZE	H. Elliott McBride	107

CONTENTS

	PAGE
WASHINGTON'S VISION—Tableau . *Amanda P. Selkrig*	113
CURING AN INVALID	115
LITTLE FOLKS' OPINIONS . . . . . *H. Elliott McBride*	119
THE DOCTOR'S CHOICE . . . . . *Alice M. Ball*	121
THE UNWELCOME GUEST . . . . *H. Elliott McBride*	126
NOT WHAT HE WANTED . . . . *J. D. Vinton*	131
SAVED—Dialogue and Tableau	139
TWO WAYS OF TELLING THE SAME THING . . . . . *Mrs. E. B. Duffey*	145
AUNT DEBBY'S SPECULATION . . . *Mrs. J. E. McConaughy*	152
ILLINOIS—Acting Charade	162
THE YOUNG DEBATERS . . . . . *H. Elliott McBride*	163
THE TWO DOLLS . . . . *Mrs. Louise E. V. Boyd*	170
THE CENSUS TAKER . . . . . *Millie M. Olcott*	173
THE RETURNED BROTHER . . . . *H. Elliott McBride*	179
AFTER A FASHION . . . . . . *Mrs. E. B. Duffey*	183
A FRIGHTENED LODGER	188

STERLING DIALOGUES

OLD HEADS ON YOUNG SHOULDERS.

CHARACTERS:—MRS. GRIMSHAW, fussy old Lady.
POLLY, her Step-daughter.
JOE, POLLY'S Brother.
FANNIE, POLLY'S Cousin.
ELIHU GOAHEAD, foppish old Gentleman.

SCENE.—MRS. GRIMSHAW, in cap and spectacles, and a letter in her hand, which she opens and reads with much apparent satisfaction.

MRS. GRIMSHAW—(*Calls*)—Polly! Polly!

Enter POLLY, *looking much frightened.*

POLLY—Well, ma'am! (*Going to sit down.*)

MRS. GRIMSHAW—Don't sit down till I give you permission. How pert you are!

POLLY—I didn't mean to be. Do you want me?

MRS. GRIMSHAW—Yes, I do want you; I want you particularly; I want you on this occasion to give me your undivided attention; I want you to be serious; I want to confide to you a subject of the greatest importance: and now you may sit down. (POLLY, *sitting down, bursts into a little laugh, but tries to conceal it by turning it into a cough.*) Why, what a cough you have to-day! You must bathe your feet, and take some red pepper tea, and put a piece of red flannel around your throat, and wear your night-cap; it is just perversity in you not to wear a night-cap—every discreet young lady does wear a night-cap; they are very becoming, too, and the broader the frill the better they look. (POLLY *again laughs, but ends by coughing.*) Oh, what a cough! It must be attended to. But now we will proceed to business. Sit up straight; fold your hands; your hair is not as smooth as it should be, your collar is a little crooked. Let me see your shoes; nothing speaks as well for a young lady's neatness as for her shoes to be neatly laced. Polly, here is a letter from my respected friend, Mr. Elihu Goahead of Goaheadville. He's as rich as a lord, and a great catch, I assure you. Yes, Polly, you might search through the world's lotteries a long while before you could draw such another prize as Mr. Elihu Goahead.

POLLY—Ha! ha! ha! Oh, what a name! what a name!

MRS. GRIMSHAW—What a name! Indeed it's a very good name.

POLLY—(*Still laughing*)—It is too funny for anything!

MRS. GRIMSHAW—Stop your laughing, you frivolous simpleton. I wont have it. Have you no propriety at all? My mother never laughed herself, and never allowed her children to, and they rewarded her care by being very proper people, very indeed. Ah! dear me, what my trials are since I became your step-mother. Just to think of a girl of sixteen laughing right in my face at the name of my friend. People can't help their names. Suppose your name was Polly Pickle, I guess you couldn't help that.

POLLY—(*Again laughing*)—No, I couldn't help it, but I'd laugh at it. Polly Pickle! I'd die laughing at that. Ha! ha! ha!

MRS. GRIMSHAW—Hush! hush! listen to me. (*Opening the letter, adjusting her glasses, and looking at* POLLY *with a severe expression.*) Here, now, is a chance for you. This old gentleman—

Polly—Old! Is he old?

Mrs. Grimshaw—He's not a boy, nor a flirt, nor a scamp, nor a fop such as you would pick, but he is my friend, respectable and responsible, Mr. Elihu Goahead.

Polly—(*Slowly*)—Mister I-like-you Go-a-head!

Mrs. Grimshaw—Polly, this is wasting time. At one o'clock my old friend—

Polly—(*In an undertone*)—Old! old!

Mrs. Grimshaw—He will be here, and I will have a splendid dinner—turkey, oysters, coffee, cakes. If you don't receive Mr. Goahead as you should, you will lose not only the offer of his heart and hand, but all the good things: for remember, I will send you to your own room and there serve you with nothing but bread and water, until you learn to be something less of a child, something less of a *tom-boy*, I may say, for a tom-boy you *are*, and it all comes of your intimacy with your hopeful cousin Fanny; understand that hereafter my doors will not be open to her, and you *sha' n't* visit her, and I'll send your brother Joe off to school. Yes, I'll revolutionize this whole concern. Your father says it's no use to try to put old heads on young shoulders; but I'll show him I can do even that! (*She flings the letter into* Polly's *lap, who reads it over, while* Mrs. Grimshaw *arrays herself in bonnet, shawl and gloves.*) Polly, I will now start for the railway station. Do you go and dress yourself neatly, and be ready to receive Mr. Goahead; and when you are established in his fine house you will thank me for all this. Be discreet for once, Polly, do be discreet for once.

Polly—Oh, to be—ha! ha! Oh, to be sure—ha! ha! ha!

[*As the old lady turns around threateningly, the laugh becomes a cough.*]

Mrs. Grimshaw—Polly, I go now; remember what I

say. You may be Mrs. Elihu Goahead if you will, or you may find yourself living on bread and water in your own room, while turkey, and oysters, and coffee, and pleasant society will be the order of the day. You must try to have an old head on young shoulders. [*Exit.*

Enter FANNY, *with a great bound, her hat flung back on her shoulders, hair in disorder, and without hoops.*

FANNY—So old Grim's gone, has she? I dodged her nicely, came in the back door as she went out of the front; but what have we here?

POLLY—Fanny, Fanny, I wish I was nobody. She has gone, but she will be back, and you must go away. She says you sha'n't come here any more.

FANNY—(*Throwing off her hat*)—But I will. This is my uncle's house, and you are my own cousin. Let's have some fun. Where's Joe? Come, brighten up.

POLLY—Fan, look here; look at this letter. She's gone now to meet this friend of hers.

FANNY—(*Glancing at the letter*)—For ever and ever! This is fine! Mr. Elihu Goahead, his name is spelled to a *T*, for it should be goat-head. A precious old hunks he must be. Is he rich?

POLLY—Rich as a Jew, and stupendously proper. I hate him.

FANNY—When did you see him? and why do you hate him?

POLLY—I never saw him; I never want to.

FANNY—Now, don't sigh or groan, or I'll leave. Just draw him on, and make fun of him. *I would;* I wish I'd half your chance for fun. I'd lead old Grim. A dance would do her good. I'd take the starch out of her. Let's have some fun; there comes Joe. Joe, here; Joe, come in and let us have a real high time! Polly is as solemn as a tombstone, all because she is to have a rich beau, a lordly, grand old soul, beautiful as the day, for all we know.

Enter JOE, *his coat badly torn.*

POLLY—O Joe, what will our ma say to that coat? how did you tear it so?

JOE—Easy enough. I saw the old *sweety* coming down street, and thought it time to scatter off; so I took to the fence, and there my coat *ketched*, and I could just hardly get away before she saw me.

FANNY—Fol de rol! who cares for a coat? I say, let us start a good romp and shake the cobwebs out of Polly's brain. Oh, we have a new play, Joe and I, such a good new play! Polly, come on, take it easy; every body has to have beaux some time. Don't fret though, Polly, till he is really here, and no help for it. Who knows? maybe the cars will run off the track or something else turn up.

JOE—Come, Polly, this is a new play. Oh, first rate! Here are some strings. Fanny, tie her hands behind her, and now we'll just show her what fun is! (*Producing strong cord, they tie* POLLY'S *hands behind her, all laughing in great glee.* JOE *looks out and says:*) My gracious, who'd 'a thought it? Dear! oh, dear!

POLLY—What is it, Joe?

JOE—The old lady and—and an old fellow along with her. This is a jolly go!

POLLY—Undo my hands!

FANNY—(*Trying hard to untie the knots*)—I can not, to save my life, loosen this!

POLLY—Oh, I'm undone, I'm undone!

JOE—No, you're not, by a good deal!

FANNY—(*Rummaging a work-basket*)—The scissors, the scissors, they're not here.

POLLY—Joe, your knife, your knife, quick.

Joe—(*Carelessly*)—I traded it for a quart of chestnuts.

Polly—(*Angrily*)—Are you both possessed? Get me loose, I say! I wont put up with this! Joe, I'll tell ma!

Joe—Ha! ha! ha! Never saw such fun in all my life. Girls in a scrape, and don't know how to get out. Our lady ma will quite forget my torn coat, when she sees Poll's predicament. (*Sings:*)

   Hey, Polly, don't you feel jolly?
   Don't you feel jolly, pretty Polly?

[Fanny, *flying at* Joe, *boxes his ears, and turns him out; he looks in once more to say:*]

Joe—They're inside the gate; I wish you a happy time of it.

Fanny—(*Soothingly*)—Polly dear, don't fret. I'll make this all right. I wasn't born in the woods to be scared by an owl. Trust me; now, here. (*Thrusting her hands through* Polly's *arms.*) See, there's nothing like a little strategy. How fortunate that I have no hoops on. You talk now, I will *do the gestures*, and get you through. There they are; be calm and cool; I am.

Mrs. Grimshaw—(*Bringing* Mr. Goahead *forward*) —Mr. Goahead, allow me the pleasure of presenting to you my daughter Polly. She is, I must assure you, Mr. Goahead, a very discreet young person. Indeed, I might say that with her I have succeeded in putting an old head on young shoulders.

Mr. Goahead—(*Approaching, shakes hands*)—Miss Polly, I am glad to see you, and you have (*Still holding her hand*), you have a very beautiful small hand. I love a small hand. (*Takes a rose from his button-hole.*) Here, Miss Polly, accept this little tribute to beauty, inhale its fragrance, and tell me if you are not an admirer of nature.

[*Here* Mrs. Grimshaw *gives* Mr. Goahead *a chair, and pushes one toward* Polly, *who seats herself in* Fanny's *lap on it.*]

Polly—(*Smelling the rose*)—I am an enthusiastic admirer of nature, Mr. Goahead. The flowers at my feet, the stars in the blue heavens above, the far-off hills, these near streams hurrying on to the ocean, all, all enchant me!

[*During this speech,* Fanny *is profuse in gestures.*]

Mr. Goahead—Upon my word, you are quite eloquent. I love eloquence. Time would pass swiftly with you, miss; but let me see, what time it is? (*Takes out his watch.*) My watch has stopped. What time have you, Miss Polly?

Polly—(*As the hands take out her watch*)—Half past two!

[*Puts the watch back, takes her handkerchief from her pocket and wipes her mouth, bursting into a little laugh, which turns to a cough.*]

Mrs. Grimshaw—(*Stamping*)—Polly, something must be done for that cough. You had better take some pepper tea, and eat nothing.

[Joe *is now seen behind* Mr. Goahead *and* Mrs. Grimshaw, *with a large butcher-knife in his hand, making signs as if to cut off the old gentleman's head, which increases* Polly's *cough, and* Mrs. Grimshaw, *growing uneasy, steps forward and calls to the cook to hurry dinner; and standing in the doorway, seems to give many directions.* Mr. Goahead *has taken up a magazine, and turning the leaves, asks:*]

Mr. Goahead—Miss Polly, here are a number of bridal costumes given; now tell me how you think a bride should be dressed.

Polly—In white, pure white, with a double skirt; and the orange blossom wreaths should be not only on the brow, but all about the flounces; and the slippers of satin;

and the veil floating around the form, should be of the finest lace; and a costly brooch of pearls should rest above the heart. (*Many gestures.*)

MR. GOAHEAD—The picture is heavenly; yes, too heavenly! Oh, how I long to gaze upon it! But, lady, let me place upon your slender finger this ring.

(*He draws it off.*)

POLLY—No, thank you; oh, no! (*He attempts it, but the hands close tight.*)

MRS. GRIMSHAW—(*Alarmed for the result, announces dinner ready, and saying, affably :*)—Mr. Goahead, give your arm to Miss Polly, and follow me. (*Goes out.*)

MR. GOAHEAD—Miss Polly, please honor me by taking my arm.

[*As he offers it, JOE steps nimbly forward, cuts the cord, and POLLY taking the old gentleman's arm, they march out, leaving FANNY and JOE standing together on the stage, looking at each other.*]

JOE—My goodness! And so this is our new play. What a one it is! What do you call it?

FANNY—"Old heads on young shoulders!"

[*Curtain.*]

JUST FROM THE CITY.

CHARACTERS:—SAM JONES, country Rustic.
ERASTUS BLINKNAT, city Swell.
EVALENA EVANS, Cousin of SAM'S.
OFFICER.

SCENE I.—A wood. SAM JONES discovered whittling.

Enter ERASTUS BLINKNAT.

ERASTUS—How do you do?

SAM—Hallo! Whar'd yeou cum from?

ERASTUS—I came down fwom the citaw. I wish to find the wesidence of Mrs. Jones. Can you assist me?

SAM—Wall, yes, I reckon I kin. I'm purty well acquainted around in these diggin's.

ERASTUS—So I supposed.

SAM—And yeou want tew go tew the house of Mrs. Jones? I reckon yeou ben't a relation of hers, be yeou?

ERASTUS—No, sir; I am not. But, weally, if you know where she wesides I'd be supwemely happy if you would infowm me. I am in somewhat of a hurwy.

SAM—Yeou don't say so! Wall, neow, if yeou ben't a relation of Mrs. Jones's I'd like tew know what on airth yeou air goin' there fur.

ERASTUS—(*Aside*)—A vewey impudent and inquisitive boaw. (*To* SAM.) I wish to infowm you, sir, that I do not desiaw to hold any further convewsation with you, unless you will give me the diwections I so much desiaw.

SAM—Sartinly, I'll give yeou all the directions yeou want. I'll tell yeou all abeout the Jones' family, and if yeou want, I'll tell yeou about the Barkers, and the Higginses, and the Wumperleys and the Scoozinhams, and all the rest of the people as lives areound here. Reckon yeov haint never been areound in these diggin's afore?

ERASTUS—No; I have nevaw had that honaw.

SAM—What makes yeou talk in that twisted sort of a way? Yeou say *honaw* and *nevaw* jest like as if thar was somethin' wrong with yeour jaws. Reckon yeou've got the mumps, or somethin'.

ERASTUS—(*Aside*)—What a disagweeably booby! (*To* SAM.) I would pwefer not to convewse with you.

SAM—Wall, neow, that's not like me, fur I like tew talk tew e'en a'most anybody. A feller ginerally feels better arter he has got a good long talk tew somebody, and as yeou have jest cum deown from the city, I want tew ax yeou a heap of things. I haint seed a feller from the city fur up'ard of six months, and that feller was so mighty stuck up I could skurcely git a word eout of him. Thar aint any use in a feller bein' so much stuck up abeout any thing, fur we don't know what is in store fur us, and when we air feelin' our biggest and lookin' our proudest we may git a *whop* that will make us feel sad and lonely all the rest of our lives.

ERASTUS—(*Aside*)—I suppose I must heaw this fellow through with his wigmawole, or find the way myself. (*To* SAM.) Look heaw, Mr. John Smith, or whatevaw youaw name is, I have lost my way. Now, I fancy—well, I know you—

SAM—Know me! Wall, neow, I kalkilate yeou don't, if yeou think my name's John Smith. My name's Jones, and yeou air a wantin' tew go tew my marm's house. The idee of me bein' a Smith! I tell yeou, sir, if yeou warn't a stranger I'd make a fuss abeout it. The Smiths aint no great shakes, and I don't take up with the idee of bein' equaled to 'em. John Smith lives deown tew Turkey Run, and he was ketched in the act of stealin' a hoss onct, so don't tell me I'm a Smith, fur I don't know as I kin allow it. Yeou know I'm a feller as can't be bamboozled and bully-ragged beyond a sartin p'int.

ERASTUS—I meant no offence. I was merely going to wemawk that I knew you—that you were one of that sowt of gentlemen as desiwed to tell his stowy through befoaw talking on any other subject. I therefoaw desiwed to say that I would heaw you through, and then you could give me the diwections so that I could find Mrs. Jones's wesidence.

SAM—Wall, yeou're a buster tew talk! I don't know as I have got any thing partickelar tew say, but I'd like tew ax yeou abeout the city. I reckon yeou have lived there fur a consid'able spell?

ERASTUS—Yes; I have been there for nearly ten yeaws.

SAM—And I reckon yeou know all the crooks and turns. Neow, I'd give a heap tew live in the city a spell. Reckon yeou wouldn't keer abeout takin' a feller with yeou when yeou go back?

ERASTUS—Well, weally I do not expect to weturn to the citaw for some time, and therefoaw it would be impossible for me to accompany you. Howevaw, you can find the way at any time. And you aw a son of Mrs. Jones, you say? I am glad I have found you. There is a young lady at youaw mothaw's house, I undewstand.

SAM—Yes; cousin Evalena's thar. Reckon yeou're her beau, aint yeou?

ERASTUS—Yes; I have that honaw. Will you conduct me to youaw wesidence, so that I may see my chawmer? If you have ever been in love you will undawstand just how I feel. I am impatient to see Miss Evalena, and I would fly on the wings of the wind to meet her.

Sam—Wall, neow, this is railly presbyterious! Here I've been a talkin' tew yeou this long spell, and never once dreamed that yeou was Evalena's beau. Thar's a feller deown here as has been tryin' tew shine areound Evalena, but I reckon she'll skurcely look at him when yeou've cum areound. Yeou air sich a stylish feller! May I ax yeour name?

Erastus—Certainly. My name is Erastus Blinknat.

Sam—And mine is Sam Jones. But I reckon yeou know all abeout our family. Evalena has told yeou, I s'pose. As I was a sayin', thar's a feller deown here as has been a shinin' reound Evalena, but I reckon it wout amount tew much. He's a mighty nice feller, but then he isn't so stylish and doesn't talk so proper and perlite. Air yeou a preacher or a lawyer?

Erastus—Neithaw.

Sam—Neither one nor t'other! Wall, neow, that's a similar sarcumstance. Yeou look as slick as a preacher. Then yeou must be a doctor?

Erastus—No; I am not a doctaw. I abhoaw medicine.

Sam—Wall, neow, if yeou aint a lawyer, nor a preacher, nor a doctor, yeou must be one of these fellers what has big stores and sells all kinds of kalikers and silks and things. Aint yeou one of them fellers?

Erastus—No, I have not that honaw.

Sam—Wall, then, I'd like tew ax yeou what yeou air? Don't yeou dew nothin'?

Erastus—No, I am happy to infowm you that I do nothing. I am a gentleman.

Sam—Land of Pequonnock! a gentleman! Wall, if that don't beat all natur'.

Erastus—Did you nevaw see a gentleman befoaw?

Sam—Yes, I kalkilate I'm one myself, but I had no idee that a gentleman was a feller as didn't dew nothin'.

Deown here we call fellers of that kind *loafers*. Reckon yeou must be a reg'lar built loafer.

ERASTUS—(*Aside*)—This fellow's impudence is dweadful. But he is a cousin of Evalena's, and I mustn't get up a wumpus with him. (*To* SAM.) Well, let us move on. I am anxious to gaze upon my chawmaw—the beautiful Evalena.

SAM—Yes, I see yeou seem tew be sorter oneasy. But thar aint no hurry. We'll git thar abeout dark, and deown here it aint fashionable to go a sparkin' till arter dark.

ERASTUS—But I flattaw myself that Evalena will be wejoiced to see me at any time of day.

SAM—Don't be too sure abeout that. Sometimes when a feller thinks he's gittin' along splendid in his courtin' he gits an awful backset. Neow thar was Azariah Harkens deown tew Goose Holler. He was a courtin' Arabella Scruggins awful strong, and he 'peared tew think that it wouldn't be of no kind of use fur another feller tew look at her; he jest thought he could git her, and no mistake. Wall, sure's yeou're born, Arabella ups one night and telled him she guessed he'd better not come any more, as it warn't no kind of use. This made Azariah feel mighty bad, and he tuck the solemnchollies, and he haint never been cout a sparkin' since.

ERASTUS—I think we had bettaw walk on, and you can tell youaw amusing stowies as we pass along.

SAM—Yes, that's so, Mr. Brickbat. Come along.

[*Exit both.*

[*Curtain.*]

SCENE II.—A room in MRS. JONES'S house. EVALENA and ERASTUS seated.

EVALENA—Mr. Blinknat, you should not have come here. I wanted time to consider the matter, and I did not wish to be disturbed.

Erastus—Well, weally, I could not wait. I found out youaw wetweat, and I felt that I must fly to you. O Evalena, beautiful woman, do not upbwaid me. I live upon youaw smiles, and I thought I must come immediately and plead for an answer.

Evalena—And you must have your answer now?

Erastus—Yes, oh, yes, answer me. Let me not pine and be unhappy. Aftaw the encouragement you have given me, you will accept me and make me a happy man.

Evalena—As you are so exceedingly desirous of an immediate answer, I will give you my answer.

Erastus—Oh, yes, youaw answer, and make me one of the happiest mowtals upon the face of the eawth. But do not cwush me—oh, no, do not cwush me!

Evalena—My answer is *No!*

Erastus—Oh, dweadful! You do not mean it?

Evalena—I do.

Erastus—Oh, unsay those cwuel words or I shall be misewable all the days of my life. O Evalena, do not kill me!

Evalena—You have my answer.

Erastus—Oh, but I can not take *no* for an answer. Oh, no, no! I can not, I can not! You will not cwush me thus when you have heawtofoaw looked upon me with such gweat favor.

Evalena—It is useless to multiply words. I have given the only answer I can give you; the only answer I *will* give you. Do you understand me?

Erastus—Oh, no, no! I can not undawstand such cwushing words. O Evalena, do not kill me!

Enter Sam *and an* Officer.

Sam—Wall, if Evalena doesn't kill yeou I kalkilate here's a feller as will.

ERASTUS—What means this intwusion?

SAM—Why, yeou see, Mr. Brickbat, this feller thinks yeou air courtin' a leetle too airnestly. When yeou find eout what he's arter I kalkilate yeou'll see a Brickbat fly.

ERASTUS—I demand an answer. What means this intwusion?

OFFICER — (*Advancing and placing his hand on* ERASTUS' *shoulder*)—I arrest you on a charge of counterfeiting.

ERASTUS—What do you mean? I demand an answer. [*Exit* EVALENA, *R.* Oh, you have dwiven her away. You shall suffaw for this. (*Breaks away from* OFFICER *and attempts to run off, L.*)

SAM—(*Seizing him*)—Wall, I kalkilate not. (*To* OFFICER.) The Brickbat did n't fly that time. (*To* ERASTUS.) Neow yeou jest keep yeour standin' or I'll fetch yeou a whop with my fist.

ERASTUS—Oh, this is excwuciating!

(OFFICER *puts on bracelets.*)

SAM—Yes, I reckon it does make yeou feel sort of cranky. But this is ginerally the case. Loafers do e'en a' most universally come to some bad eend.

ERASTUS—You stupid fool, shut up.

SAM—Why, Mr. Brickbat, yeou seem tew be takin' a spell of the tantarantums.

OFFICER—Come along; we can't stand here all day.

SAM—I say, Mr. Brickbat, when yeou git eout, cum deown ag'in. Fetch yeour knittin' and stay awhile!

[*Exit* ERASTUS *and* OFFICER. That's jest the way it turns eout with these fellers as doesn't like tew work. Wall, I reckon I'd better step eout and say good-bye tew the Brickbat. [*Exit* SAM.

[*Curtain.*]

TRUSTY AND TRUE.

CHARACTERS:—MR. SOULE, a Merchant.
JOHN RUSSELL, }
FRANK GREY, } Clerks.
AMASA DREW, }

SCENE I.—Counting room. RUSSELL seated at a desk, busy with a day-book and ledger.

Enter DREW *and* GREY *unperceived by him.*

RUSSELL—(*Speaking to himself*)—There you are! I've conquered you at last. All those long columns of figures are right, sir! Now, John Russell, I think a page of algebra will get the cobwebs out of your brain. So here's at it, my boy!

DREW—(*Slapping him on the shoulder*)—So, here's your den, where you hide yourself, old fellow! What a fool you are, to work two hours after the rest are out!

GREY—And now he talks about *algebra!* I'd go sailing up Salt River, with a sign over me, before *I'd* touch an algebra. Sure enough, what *do* you stay here for so late o' nights?

RUSSELL—Well, to-night I stayed to do a little work for Mr. Soule—a few figures that somehow would n't add up right. But I've balanced every thing all straight; and I'm glad of it. They were in a snarl, somewhat, but it's all right.

DREW—And the algebra?

RUSSELL—Oh, you know Mr. Soule told us the other day he must do with less help soon. And as I'm the youngest clerk, I expect to be the one to be turned off. So I'm brushing up a little. Just to prepare for a winter campaign of teaching. That's all.

GREY—(*Putting his hands in his pockets, and looking solemnly at* RUSSELL)—Russell, how old are you?

Russell—(*Smiling*)—Oh, I'm almost eighteen. Rather young, I know; but I taught last winter with pretty good success. I'll do better this year.

Grey—Well, I'm glad you aren't quite a hundred. A fellow 'd think, though, to hear you talk, that you came out of the ark.

Drew—Looks arkish, doesn't he, Frank? Well, one thing *I* know. You're a fool to work over your hours for old Soule. He doesn't pay you extra.

Russell—I don't ask anything for a little kindness like that. Mr. Soule is a kind, considerate employer, and does a great deal for us, *you* know. I'm glad to do him any little favor, I'm sure.

Grey—Well, old fellow, don't stay here moping all the evening. It's a splendid night! Come with us and have some fun.

Russell—What kind of fun?

Grey—Oh, most any thing. A hand at euchre, perhaps.

Russell—My dear fellow, I don't know one card from another. In the ark, where I was brought up, cards are *non est*.

Drew—Of course. Well, say a game of billiards, for variety.

Russell—I am not going to the billiard-room again. I confess to a fondness for the game, but they make it a regular gambling operation; and such a set of profane, half-drunken rowdies as they get in. *No, sir!* I beg to be excused. I wish you wouldn't go, boys.

Drew—*I've* no conscientious scruples, and I'm not afraid. *I* wasn't brought up in the ark, thank fortune.

Russell—Mine was a blessed, restful, safe old ark, thank Heaven! The memory of it has been a safeguard in many a temptation.

Grey—Yes, yes, no doubt! You make me home-sick; for your words bring to mind *my* dear old home in the country.

Drew—There, boys, don't be spoonies! We'll just go it while we're young, and have a good time. See here, Russell, we came in to ask you to take a sail with us to-morrow. There's a party of us going over to the island—it's going to be a splendid day!

Russell—You don't mean to-morrow! To-morrow's Sunday! You've forgotten.

Drew—Forgotten! Just as if it could be any harm for us poor fellows, who are shut up within brick walls six days out of seven, to take a sail on Sunday!

Grey—You can go to church twice and attend your Sunday-school, and then go. That wouldn't be breaking the Sabbath.

Drew—Come, Russell, do go just for once! I tell you Diamond Island is just splendid now. Come!

Russell—Stop a moment. Let me think. I tell you, boys, *I'd like* to go! I've been in the city ten months, and all the country I've seen is that pitiful little Common, and the bit of green in front of my boarding house. I'd like to go, if it was right, but—

Grey—Hurra! "The man that deliberates is lost." He'll go, Drew; we only want him to complete our number. We'll have a gay old time.

Russell—See here, boys, don't be too fast. Just let me read you a part of my mother's last letter. (*Takes a letter from his breast pocket, and opens it.*) You see, I carry it next my heart. (*Reads:*) "I hope, my child, you will never be tempted to spend any portion of the Sabbath in a way that your mother would not approve. I know you must be lonely on that day, and that you must miss us all. But do not forget that day *belongs to*

God. You can not expect His blessing, if you do not 're-member the Sabbath.'" Now, boys, you see I sat right down and wrote to mother that I wouldn't *be* tempted to do any thing on the Sabbath that she wouldn't like me to do. So you see I can't go.

Grey—Well, you needn't preach any more. We'll get enough of that to-morrow.

Russell—I beg your pardon, boys. I think I never intruded my opinions upon you before. But, honest, I don't think it right to go sailing on Sunday.

Grey—And, honest, I don't—so there!

Russell—Oh, then, be true to your conscience, and don't go.

Grey—I've promised, and I must this once. But it shall be the *very last time.*

Drew—Hold your tongue, Grey, and don't be a fool. Russell, you've always been a clever fellow, never poking your nose into other folks' business, and you've never "let on" about us fellows that don't think as you do. I respect you for it. And now I want you to do us a favor, will you?

Russell—Certainly, if I can.

Drew—Well, you can. Tell us where old Soule keeps the key to his boat-house.

Grey—You are not supposed to mistrust what we want to know for.

Drew—Oh, we want to know just for information. We have inquiring minds, you see. A little curiosity—that's all.

Russell—But I *do* suspect your intentions. You want to get Mr. Soule's " Favorite " to go sailing with to-morrow.

Drew—Granted. He's a stingy old scamp. He wont let his boat, and there isn't another to be had, for love or money. All you've got to do about it is to say, accidentally, where he keeps the key. We know you have charge of it.

RUSSELL—(*Walking about, as if thinking, and then speaking*)—Can you keep a secret, boys?

DREW—Mum's the word. Nobody shall ever know. The rack couldn't wring it from us.

GREY—Oh, yes; we can keep a secret, and we will. Let us have it.

RUSSELL—*So can I;* and so I will! Mr. Soule gave me the care of the boat-house key. I promised him I would neither let it go out of my possession, nor tell where I keep it. I know you'll both be offended, but I can't help it. My motto is "*trusty and true*," and I'll stick to it as long as I live.

DREW—You're a booby, spooney, and coward! I cut your acquaintance for ever. (*Goes out.*)

GREY—(*Following* DREW, *takes* RUSSELL'S *hand, and speaks in a low voice.*)—I respect you, Russell. I don't blame you! Don't forget me.

RUSSELL—Well, they've gone. Heigho! I've made a life-time enemy; but I can't help it! I'm a booby and a spooney, may be, but I'm not a coward. I know I'd rather march up to the cannon's mouth than to face such music as this. Oh, dear! wouldn't I like to have somebody tell me I'm *not* a booby. I wish somebody cared about us poor stranger-boys. When I'm a man, I'll hunt up all the young fellows, and just let them see that somebody has an interest in them. I'll ask them to church and Sabbath-school and—ah! well! that's another of my foolish notions. I suppose I *must* be a little unfinished in the upper story. I'll off to bed and to sleep. [*Exit.*

[*Curtain.*]

SCENE II.—Place same as before. Time, Monday morning. MR. SOULE sitting by a desk.

Enter RUSSELL.

RUSSELL—You wished to see me, sir?

SOULE—Ah, Russell! (*Extending his hand.*) Glad to see you so prompt! Sit down here. I want to have a little talk with you.

RUSSELL—(*Taking a seat*)—Thank you, sir, I've been expecting this for a week. I suppose you're about to make the change you spoke of. I'm sorry to go, sir, but as I'm the youngest clerk, I expected to be the first one turned off.

SOULE—Yes, I am making some changes in my business, and some two or three must be discharged. You found the snarl here, (*Laying his hand on the ledger,*) and unraveled it, I see.

RUSSELL—Yes, sir; I think it is all right.

SOULE—All right, Russell, and *very* well done. Have you seen Drew this morning?

RUSSELL—No, sir; neither Drew nor Grey. I wondered where they are to-day. I noticed neither of their desks were filled.

SOULE—Then you haven't heard the news?

RUSSELL—No, sir! What news?

SOULE—Frank Grey had his eye put out last night, in a billiard saloon, in a drunken quarrel!

RUSSELL—Frank Grey! Poor fellow! You don't mean to say *he* had been drinking, Mr. Soule?

SOULE—No, I think not. He got mixed up in the quarrel somehow. It is a great pity he was ever tempted to go there at all. Grey is not very wicked yet, only a little weak.

RUSSELL—Perhaps this may save him. I hope so.

He's good-hearted. Poor Frank! Lost an eye! How terrible!

Soule—Yes, but it might have been worse. If the loss of an eye will reform his character and make his life useful, it will be a mercy, after all. There's another piece of bad news which I presume you haven't heard. Drew is in the lockup.

Russell—(*Astonished*)—In the *where?*

Soule—In "durance vile," Russell, on the charge of breaking and entering.

Russell—Whose store? *Can* it be true, Mr. Soule?

Soule—Captain Nelson's boat-house. He stole Nelson's yacht, he and some other fellows, and went pleasuring. Nelson's angry, of course, and had them arrested this morning.

Russell—It is a sad thing! I am very sorry. Was Grey one of the party?

Soule—No, he wasn't. He had a sick headache all day, and it is a great pity it hadn't lasted all the evening, as well.

Russell—Somebody coaxed him off. The poor fellow could never say "no."

Soule—It's a great pity. The fact is, he isn't "*trusty and true.*" Very few young men are. When I find one that is, I consider him worth his weight in diamonds—eh, John?

Russell—Yes, sir; I suppose so, sir! That is, my parents always taught me so.

Soule—Don't blush so, Russell, my dear fellow. I didn't mean to play eaves-dropper last Saturday night, but I heard your conversation with Drew and Grey. You have been well taught, and you do your parents honor. You shall not suffer for your defence of me and my property, I assure you.

Russell—I only did my duty, sir. When do you want me to leave—to-day?

Soule—I don't wish you to leave at all.

Russell—I thought you said—

Soule—You mustn't jump at conclusions. I said I was about making some change, and I am. I sent for you to offer you the clerkship made vacant by Drew. That gives you a jump over four years, and will more than double your salary.

Russell—O Mr. Soule, how can I thank you? Do you think I am competent to do his work!

Soule—I *think* so. That was his work you righted up on Saturday night.

Russell—Mr. Soule, you never can know what you have done for us all—mother and sister and me. I hope you will *never* have cause to regret your kindness.

Soule—I never shall, if you continue *trusty and true*. That is all I ask of you. For no man can be that to the full, without being more—a true Christian.

(*He shakes* Russell's *hand, and exits.*)

Russell—(*Pinching himself*)—It isn't me. I must be dreaming. John Russell, the booby, spooney, coward! O mother, it all comes of your teaching! And earnestly will I pray that I be not led into temptation, but ever be trusty and true.

[*Curtain.*]

UNAPPRECIATED GENIUS.

CHARACTERS:—Mr. BROWN.
MRS. BROWN.
ALPHONSE, } small Boys.
ADOLPHUS,
CLEMENTINA, little Girl.
BIDDY, Domestic.

SCENE.—Disordered room; everything in confusion.

Enter MRS. BROWN, *with knotted hair and soiled dress. Takes up manuscript and looks it over.*

MRS. BROWN—Dear, dear! Here it is Saturday morning, and that article for the *Hardscrabble News* not finished yet. Let me see! How did it read? (*Reads aloud:*) "On a beautiful day in the leafy month of June, when all nature was bursting forth with—"

Enter BIDDY.

BIDDY—Ungyuns, mum! Will ye be havin' them for dinner, mum?

MRS. BROWN—Oh no, Biddy, they smell so badly. I guess we'll have the bits left from yesterday's dinner *hashed* for to-day; you know Mr. Brown's never particular.

BIDDY—(*Aside*)—More's the pity, says I. Poor mon! (*To* MRS. BROWN.) The bits is all gone, mum. Give 'em to the dog, mum, to Bounce.

MRS. BROWN—Oh, Biddy, how could you! Enough for two good dinners! I haven't time to go down to the pantry; can't you *tell* me what there is?

BIDDY—That I can, mum, fur me two eyes can say, an' me two hands can hold ivery bit of aitin' there is in this house, to be sure! The two boys, mum, has et up the black raisin cake—

Mrs. Brown—All my fruit-cake?

Biddy—Truth, mum, though I make bold to say it tasted strong of *merlasses* to me; Ellen Ryan says—

Mrs. Brown—What *else* is there? (*Goes to writing.*) Any bread?

Biddy—No, mum! Baby's et *that*.

Mrs. Brown—Five loaves baked yesterday. Poor Baby! Well, get—get—oh, something! Make a pudding, can't you? Run down and buy some bread, and some meat—steak I guess, that'll cook the quickest—and tell 'em to put it on the book.

Biddy—On the book, is it? And if it's all the same to yes, mum, I'll bring it in the basket!

Mrs. Brown—(*Laughs*)—Oh, Biddy! I mean, tell them to *charge* it to Mr. Brown.

Biddy—Yes, mum. [*Exit.*

Mrs. Brown—If Charles only would look after the help more, I would be glad; he must see that *I* don't get time. Her mother was here yesterday, and that accounts for empty larder, the children never touch anything, *precious* ones. Oh, dear! (*Yawns, and reads again:*) "Nature was bursting forth with all her wealth of—"

Enter Alphonse, *and* Clementina.

Alphonse—(*Holding up his buttonless jacket*)—Buttons all off my jacket, mamma; see!

Mrs. Brown — (*Abstractedly*) — Pin it, Alphonse. (*Reads:*) "wealth of buds, and—"

Alphonse—Apple, mamma, Clementina's got my apple.

Clementina—Just *one* bite, mamma.

Mrs. Brown—Give it to brother, dear; run and play, and you may take my white *crêpe* shawl.

Clementina—Your very bestest one, mamma. You

nodded us yes. Oh, you're just the sweetest, (*Kisses her rapturously,*) goodest mamma.

Mrs. Brown—Run away, pet, you'll stick my face all up with your apple. (*Reads:*) "blossoms to gladden weary man. The sun was slowly sinking in a—"

[*Exit both.*

Enter Biddy.

Biddy—Swill-pail, mum! Baby's fell in it, sure; he's kickin' an' squallin' awful, mum.

Mrs. Brown—Get him out quick, and take off his dress. Poor baby.

Biddy—Yes, mum. [*Exit.*

Mrs. Brown—(*Reads*)—"blazing radiance—"

Enter Alphonse, Adolphus *and* Clementina.

Alphonse—Fire's all out, mamma; mayn't me, and 'Dolph, and Clem come in where you be?

Mrs. Brown—What grammar! What manners! No, dears; run out and skate, mamma's busy. Put on your mittens.

Alphonse—The strap to my skate's broke.

Mrs. Brown—Take a string, can't you? [*Exit all.* (*Reads:*) "in a blazing radiance of glory, when a stranger might have been seen approaching a—"

Enter Biddy.

Biddy—Beef's liver; all the meat he had, mum.

Mrs. Brown—Dreadful! Fix it someway.

Biddy—Yes, mum. [*Exit.*

Mrs. Brown—(*Reads*)—"approaching a dwelling on outskirts of a small village. He was seated on a—"

Enter Biddy.

Biddy—Clothes-line's broke, mum, an' let the beautiful white clothes, as white as your own hand, missis, right down on the dirty ground, an' me so tired, what with doin' iverything, that I've no strength lift at all, 'tall, an' twelve of the clock and no dinner.

Mrs. Brown—I'm sorry; can't you take the bedford?

Biddy—(*Aside*)—Little does the likes of her care if me fingers wuz worked off to me elbows.

Mrs. Brown—(*Reads*)—" Sitting on a—"

Enter Adolphus.

Adolphus—(*Riding a broom-handle, calls out noisily*)—Horse, mamma, has comed right into your house! Don't you touch him, mamma, or he'll kick. (*Sings:*) "I'll bet my money—"

Mrs. Brown—Stop, sir! Where does he get that slang? Leave the room this minute! (*He goes off crying.*) —"on a noble steed who seemed proudly conscious of its—"

Enter Clementina.

Clementina—(*With doll*)—Eyes all bunged out; mamma, (*crying,*) my baby's spoilt!

Mrs. Brown—Go out, and close the door!

[*Exit* Clementina.

(*Reads:*) "beauty and worth. As he sauntered slowly up to the humble paling, a man rushed wildly out, frantically exclaiming—"

Enter Mr. Brown.

Mr. Brown—Wife, do you know what that great blundering thing has done? Actually taken off the dear little thing's dress, as you told her, and *left* him so! Mercury at fifteen degrees below zero. I declare *my* baby sha'n't be treated so!

Mrs. Brown—(*Amiably*)—*Whose* baby? Say *our* baby, dear! If there's any one thing I dislike more than another, it is to hear a *married* man say "my this," or "my that." If I had *my* way, that word should be entirely stricken out of the domestic calendar. "Our" sounds so much more generous.

Mr. Brown—Meanwhile, will your majesty please to inform me what I shall put on to *our* shivering, neglected baby?

Mrs. Brown—Oh, wrap him up in one of the boys' roundabouts till his dress gets dry! (*He goes out.*) How little incentive a married woman feels for literary pursuits with no encouragement! Charles, too, has great intellect, but he *will* insist that "healing the sick" is of more importance than feeding the mind; I wouldn't mind it so much, only it takes him away from home most of the time, and he can't amuse the children, or oversee the house as much as he ought; but, after all, bless him; there never was so good a husband, if he can't always appreciate my flights of intellect. Where was I? (*Reads:*)—"exclaiming, 'Help, sir! Help! My wife is dying, and I—'"

Enter Mr. Brown.

Mr. Brown—Can't find *our* best pants, wife!

Mrs. Brown—(*Dreamily*)—Have you looked in the wood-box? Seems to me I saw 'em.

Mr. Brown—*Wood*-box?

Mrs. Brown—No! 'twasn't either. I put 'em into the south parlor window, where the glass is out.

Mr. Brown—What economy! (*Goes out.*)

Mrs. Brown—(*Reads*)—"Hurriedly our hero alighted, and stepping into—"

Enter Mr. Brown.

Mr. Brown—(*Hastily*)—Best hat ruined, Jane; those wretched young ones had it out on the ice for a gunboat. I do wish you would leave writing, and see to things.

Mrs. Brown—(*Soothingly*)—Biddy will. You don't feel right well to-day, do you, dear? I wouldn't call 'em young ones; they wont think you love 'em—little angels.

Mr. Brown—*Destroying* angels, I should say.

Mrs. Brown—Now, Charles, don't! You know if *you* took one-half the interest in our home affairs that *I* do, things wouldn't be so disorderly.

Mr. Brown—(*Sotto voce*)—*As much interest!*

Mrs. Brown—Don't repeat my words, dear; it isn't good taste; I—

Enter Biddy.

Biddy—Would ye be good enough, mum, to come down and set yer two eyes on till this very same puddin', mum? Och, bad luck to the day I iver tried the same! I was thinkin' could I make one loike me cousin Ann Flynn did the ither day after mass; she that married Mike Flannigan, yer mind,—

Mrs. Brown—Talk faster.

Biddy—Faster, is it? when me poor tongue is that burrunt with tastin' of the ugly hot stuff, what is no puddin' at all, 'tall, only scalt milk and bread bits.

Mrs. Brown—Did you remember the eggs and sugar?

Biddy—And it's not the loikes o' me, mum, as would be forgetting of any sich things, with me best of characters from my former missis, but I says to myself, says I: Poor mon, he little knows how things is goin' on unbeknownst to him—blessed lamb! and he gone, and I'll save him in what small ways I can, says I, and so I l'aves out—fearin' it might not be fit atin', yer see, if it didn't coom good—the sugar and eggs both of 'em—

Mr. Brown—What a goose!

Mrs. Brown—(*At the same time*)—Left 'em out? (*Both laugh.* Biddy *flounces out mad.*) Leave me just a minute till I finish this. Oh, dear, there are those noisy children. (*He goes out.*) Let me see, (*Reads:*)—"stepping into the—"

Enter MR. BROWN.

MR. BROWN—Baby's swallowed a whistle, quick!

MRS. BROWN—Oh, dear! (*Leaving room.*) Jerk up his arm! Hold his head down! Spat him on the back! Oh, my precious, precious baby! [*Exit both*

[*Curtain.*]

THE DISCONTENTED GIRLS.

CHARACTERS:—JENNIE, FLORA, } two little Girls.

SCENE.—FLORA and JENNIE standing, with dirty faces, tangled hair, shoe-strings untied; one with a bonnet on, and the other swinging hers in her hand; and each carrying a load of school books.

JENNIE—So, you are ready for school, are you? I see you have got your bonnet and books.

FLORA—Yes, I 'spose I've got to go, whether I want to or not. The plagued old school! I don't care a cent for it. All I do is get scolded! When I am at home, mother scolds all the time; and when I am at school, the teacher scolds. It's scold, scold, scold, all the whole time, from daylight till darkness! I am glad when it's time to go to bed, so I wont hear any more scolding; and I tell you, I lie as late in the morning as possible. Mother keeps calling me to get up, but I know how to fix *her*. I just stuff the bed-clothes in my ears, just as tight as I can; and then she calls, and calls, and I never hear a single word!

JENNIE—That's just the way I do, too! I look out how I get up before breakfast! I can do work enough afterwards, and get scolding enough too. I have to hold the baby all the time, and all he does is squall, and then mother scolds, but I do n't care! I make him squall sometimes, on purpose! I hate babies, and I would n't take care of them if I could help it! I am glad when school-time comes, so as to get away from them. It's not quite so bad there, but it's bad enough, for it's study, study, study! I can't look off the book a single minute, but the teacher sees me; and then those terrible geography lessons, with all those long hard names. I can *never* learn them. I suppose I shall have to stay after school every night, but I do n't know as I care.

Flora—I just know what I wish. I wish I was a grown-up young lady. I would go to all the dances, and parties, I wanted to. I guess I'd do as I pleased then! I'd have just as many dresses as I wanted. I'd not wear an old flannel dress like this; and I'd have such beautiful feathers, and ribbons; Oh, I'd cut a dash, I tell you!

[*Exit both together.*]

[*Curtain.*]

COLORADO.

AN ACTING CHARADE.

CHARACTERS:—Teacher, young Lady.
Seven Children, her Pupils.

Scene:—A noisy school-room. Scholars standing. Teacher rings bell, and they take their seats.

First Scholar—(*Points to* Teacher's *collar, loose at one end*)—Look at her *collar!* (*Whispering.*)

Second Scholar—Will, I've got your tag.

Third Scholar—(*To* Fourth Scholar)—Where's the red apple you promised to bring me?

Fourth Scholar—(*To* Third Scholar)—I've *et it* up.

Teacher—Order, order!

Fifth Scholar—(*Catching* Teacher *by dress*)—Teacher, your collar is unpinned!

First Scholar—Your *collar!*

Sixth Scholar—I've got a pin!

Teacher—I'd like the lessons better learned than they were yesterday.

Seventh Scholar—Hadn't you better fix your *collar!*

Teacher—Yes; I'll fix my collar! Now, first thing, we'll have an exercise in orthography. All give second sound of *a*. (*All give different sounds of a.*)

Teacher—Horrible! Second sound, I said; try again. (*Some give e and some u.*)

Teacher—No; give it like this. (*Sounds ă. All give it with great stress.*)

Teacher—Perhaps singing will go better. Order! Turn to the fourth page of singing books. Now all sing *Do*. (*Each one takes a different key.*)

Fifth Scholar—Will is singing *Bass*.

Third Scholar—Tom's got *Tenor*.

Fourth Scholar—Which is mine, *Air* or *Second!*

Teacher—*All* sing with *me!* (*Sings Do. All sound wrong key again.*)

Teacher—Outrageous! We'll have recess.

[*Exit all.*

[*Curtain.*]

A PAIR OF LIONS.

CHARACTERS:—NED STONE, a waggish Lawyer.
  DEACON GREEN, his Cousin, a credulous Rustic.
  SENATOR FLURRY, a verbose Coward.

SCENE.—STONE'S office. Table back center, with books, etc. Chair at table. Two chairs right and left, front center.

Enter NED STONE.

NED—(*Taking off hat and coat and sitting at table*)—What a trying life we lawyers lead, to be sure—trying always as hard as possible to kill the time; it's a troublesome task I find it sometimes. Heigh-ho! I'll set the first two men I come across to quarrelling and then offer my professional services. Hum! My appointment-book must be looked to. (*Takes blank-book from table.*) Let me see; it will never do to have these pages look so bare, so down go Messrs. Brown, Jones, Smith and Robinson again for the fourth time, with the addition of Mr. Ferguson. (*Writing.*) There, that looks more professional, I think. Hallo! Here's an actual letter for me, and, bless me, it's from that intensely rural cousin of mine, Zachariah Green, of Squash Hollow. (*Opens and reads.*) "Respected cousin Stone:—I am about to take the liberty of dropping in upon you as I'm a coming down to your city afore long as I want to see the sights and as I aint never been there before but once and as I am now Deacon to our meetin'-house and as I am in haste your humble servant cousin Zachariah Green. *P. S.*—I'll be after this right smart." What *have* I done to incur this affliction? Coming down upon me to see the "sights" when I am tired of everybody and every thing. Sights, eh? Well, I *will* show him the sights until he'll wish himself back at home before he's been here an hour. And there's that everlasting Senator Flurry coming in to see me this morning about his anti-something speech; he's another detestable bore; but I have a plan to get rid of them both, and I'll use it too.

Enter DEACON GREEN.

DEACON GREEN—Good morning, cousin Stone; how-de-do? I'm proud and happy to see ye. Quite a surprise now, I tell ye. Oh, lor! No it aint nuther, 'cause it's me what's a come to see ye; now aint it?

NED—Delighted to see you, cousin Zach. I've just received your letter, so that you quite surprised me.

DEACON GREEN—Wall, now, it's harnsome of ye to say so, cousin Ned. Ye'll let me call ye cousin Ned, wont ye?

NED—Certainly, why not? We're cousins, aren't we?

DEACON GREEN—So we be, so we be! Cousins now, aint we? So we be. Purty slick trade, eh, cousin Ned?

NED—Fair, for the season. Take a chair, Zach.

DEACON GREEN—Couldn't think of robbin' ye, cousin Ned; howsomdever, I don't object to sottin' down. (*Sits.*) Jiminy! This air a purty slick bit of furnetor, aint it, cousin Ned? Now I s'pose sich a chair as this cost most three dollars, wouldn't it now?

NED—Almost as much as that.

DEACON GREEN—Sho! Ye don't tell me? I say, cousin Ned, I aint interruptin' business, be I?

NED—Not a bit; my clients rarely come so early.

DEACON GREEN—Your what, don't?

NED—My clients.

DEACON GREEN—Ah, so so! But I say, cousin Ned, where'll a feller go to see the sights?

NED—You needn't stir out of your chair, one of the biggest lions in town is coming here this morning.

DEACON GREEN—How ye talk! Jerusha! I should think ye kept a hull menagerum. Say, will he bite?

NED—He does sometimes, and roars tremendously, too.

DEACON GREEN—*Ex*-cuse me; I'd rather see 'em to Barnum's.

NED—You don't understand me; this lion is a man, a most noted character in town; in fact, he's the most celebrated pugilist in the state.

DEACON GREEN—A what-ilist?

NED—A pugilist, a prize-fighter.

DEACON GREEN—Oh! I thought it might be something like a client.

NED—Well, he's coming here, and you must talk to him.

DEACON GREEN—What! Me, me, Deacon Zachariah Green, talk to a prize-fighter? Ye make my blood run cold.

NED—But you mustn't say anything against the prize-ring; he's very sensitive on the subject, and although he pretends to denounce all rings, yet he's a monomaniac in their support.

DEACON GREEN—(*Aside*)—Another critter from Barnum's, I reckon.

NED—You must favor rings with all your might, but you must not let him say too much; talk all you can yourself; he's very bloodthirsty when excited.

DEACON GREEN—Goodness gracious! I'm all in a shiver.

NED—You must not refuse to do anything he asks; if you do, he will crush you on the spot; he has already annihilated seventeen men.

DEACON GREEN—Oh, Jiminy! Deacon Zachariah Green, in scattered fragerments!

NED—Let me caution you against one thing more;

when he begins to pull down his upper lip, you will know that his blood is getting up; to quiet him, you must immediately respond by jerking his ear; he will probably then pull your nose; but keep calm, and he wont hurt you much.

Deacon Green—Oh, dear! Oh, dear! I wish I'd stayed to hum! Say, cousin Ned, I don't want to see the pugifist.

Ned—But you must; he's coming up stairs now. Get into my private room, and come out when I begin to whistle.

Deacon Green—(*Aside*)—Oh, Jiminy! Lions, and clients, and pugifists, and money-monkeys, and goodness knows what! Why *did* I come to see the sights! [*Exit.*

Ned—Ha! ha! ha! He's the easiest game I ever saw. Why, he believes that I keep a whole menagerie, and as for that Senator Flurry, he is the worst coward in town. Zach will regard him as a sanguinary prize-fighter; that's his nickname too, by-the-way. That was a lucky thought of mine, in speaking of his pulling down his lip; it's a favorite trick of his. Now for preparing the worthy Senator for an original sensation.

Enter Senator Flurry.

Ned—And how does my honorable friend find himself this morning?

Senator Flurry—Your honorable friend finds himself in a state of indignation bordering on frenzy; in fact, it is only the strong arm of the law that prevents my slaying a fellow-creature.

Ned—You positively alarm me! Who has been so heedless as to incur the enmity of so righteously vindictive a man as yourself?

Senator Flurry—You may well say vindictive; I

am a terrible enemy, when roused to action. My dear Stone, did you ever see me roused to action?

NED—My memory fails me.

SENATOR FLURRY—Ah, but you should! You should! You've read my speech against the Light House Ring—my anti-humbug speech?

NED—Every word of it.

SENATOR FLURRY—It raised a tremendous wind.

NED—Indeed it did. (*Aside.*) All noise and bluster!

SENATOR FLURRY—And yet, after crushing Senator Bombast, he has the impudence to reply, advocating the very fraud I denounced, and here's his speech in this morning's paper. It's monstrous! (*Hands paper.*)

NED—Enormous! (*Glances at it, and lays it aside.*) But I say, my dear Flurry, you must permit me to introduce to you a new lion, just arrived in town; a celebrated man, I assure you, though rather eccentric.

SENATOR FLURRY—Delighted to meet all the lions, I am sure. Is he approachable at present?

NED—Oh, yes; he's in the next room; he's an actor, and inimitable in his line; you would think that he was acting all the time, to watch him.

SENATOR FLURRY—I should like to see him perform.

NED—Nothing will please him more than to have you ask him to give you a specimen; but he pretends modesty, and you must urge him very hard; give him no opportunity to refuse.

SENATOR FLURRY—I promise you I will not.

NED—He's a little queer in his head, and his temper is something remarkable.

SENATOR FLURRY—Indeed?

NED—Yes; he will fight, on the least provocation. To keep him quiet, you must first ask him to declaim; then, to please him, denounce all church officers; he hates them all, especially deacons. At all events, don't let him talk too much or he will get ferocious, and keep close to him; if he gets beyond control, gently pull his nose; it will do him good.

SENATOR FLURRY—An original character, truly. But are all these precautions necessary?

NED—Oh, entirely so; unless you wish to be eaten alive.

SENATOR FLURRY—No, thank you. (*Aside.*) I wish I were out of this!

NED—(*Whistling*)—I think he's coming in now. Remember to act boldly, or he will challenge you on the spot.

Enter DEACON GREEN, *nervously.*

NED—(*Going to him*)—You must let me call you Roscius.

DEACON GREEN—Say, cousin Ned, I want to go home!

NED—Hush! Keep your courage up; act boldly, or he will demolish you on the spot.

DEACON GREEN—(*Aside*)—My! How wild he looks!

SENATOR FLURRY—(*Aside*)—What a ferocious character.

NED—Gentlemen, it gives me pleasure to introduce two such popular lions to each other. Mr. Roscius, Mr. Flurry: Mr. Flurry, Mr. Roscius.

SENATOR FLURRY—(*Quickly*)—Enthusiastically emotionalized at grasping you by the hand.

(*Shakes hands vigorously.*)

DEACON GREEN—That's perlite, I'm sure. I'm the same way myself, with a respect to your superior fist. (*Aside.*) Jerusha! What a grip!

SENATOR FLURRY—Your reputation is only excelled by your ability. (*Aside.*) What a capital actor!

DEACON GREEN—So it is! So it is, Mr. Pugi—I mean Mr. Fussy! I—I—I—

Senator Flurry—Capital! Capital! My dear sir, I never saw such a power of imitation.

Deacon Green—I agree with ye, squire. I'm right up with ye. (*Aside.*) I mustn't disagree, or he'll chaw me up!

Ned—Gentlemen, may I ask you to excuse me, as business demands my time? I know that you will be excellent company for each other.

(*Goes to one side, where he can watch.*)

Deacon Green—(*Aside*)—Oh, lor! He's left me with the money-monkey. Wall, I must talk, I s'pose. (*Aloud.*) I hope business is good, squire?

Senator Flurry—There's nothing particular on just now, except a little sparring between Bombast and myself.

Deacon Green—He's in the ring, hey?

Senator Flurry—Yes; he *is* in the ring.

Deacon Green—I reckon ye polished him off? (*Aside.*) That's the way these pugilists talk, I guess.

Senator Flurry—Yes; I knocked him completely off his feet.

Deacon Green—Sho! (*Aside.*) He'll serve me same way, mebbe.

Senator Flurry—I hope we shall hear you in public, before long?

Deacon Green—Wall, I may say somethin' in meetin'.

Senator Flurry—Capital acting! Capital! (*Aside.*) If I didn't know, I should say he was a genuine Yankee.

Deacon Green—So it is, squire! So it is! (*Aside.*) I wonder what on airth he's talkin' abeout!

Senator Flurry—Your life on the boards must have brought you a queer experience.

Deacon Green—Wall, no, not 'xactly; my dad, he run a saw-mill, and I did larn a little of the business.

Senator Flurry—You're inclined to facetiousness.

Deacon Green—No, I aint, squire; I'm all right; there aint nothing the matter with me.

Senator Flurry—Ha, ha! Capital! You'll draw a big house.

Deacon Green—Reckon I can, squire. I drawed Jonese's house from down 'side the grist mill, way up top of Pumpkin Hill; me and my oxen done it alone.

Senator Flurry—Delicious! Your humor is refreshing.

Deacon Green—No it aint, not a bit of it. (*Aside.*) What's he a-drivin' at, anyway?

Senator Flurry—Oh, but it is, it is! I insist upon it.

Deacon Green—So it is, so it is! if ye insist. (*Aside.*) He's gettin' ready to punch me, I know.

Senator Flurry—Now if I had a little wit like yours, to use against these *rings*.

Deacon Green—Ye can't possibly mean against the ring, squire; the ring is a noble institution—

Senator Flurry—Sir; monstrous!

Deacon Green—Ye can't possibly speak agin it; it's the right of every citizen to fight in the ring and for the ring, as you, who are the best man in the ring, the leader of all rings—

Senator Flurry—Sir—I—

Deacon Green—I can't hear ye speak agin it. (*Aside.*) Keep it up, Zachariah! Keep it up! (*Aloud.*) No, squire, ye may pretend modesty, but it wont work with me, for I know what a champion ye be in the ring. Long life to it, then. (*Aside.*) There, I'm safe!

Senator Flurry—(*Aside*)—He's verging on the ferocious! (*Aloud.*) My dear Roscius, your ardor does you credit; you would fill my place with your oratorical powers and put me to the blush.

Deacon Green—No; I aint much on my pugifist.

Senator Flurry—(*Aside*)—Some theatrical term, probably. (*Aloud.*) I must entreat you to give me a specimen of your dramatic powers; a selection from Shakspeare, or some simple little poem.

Deacon Green—Poem? I don't know no poem.

Senator Flurry—You're too modest! Your brain must be teeming over with gems.

Deacon Green—I aint much troubled that way.

Senator Flurry—But you must give me something. I insist. You must! You shall!

Deacon Green—Wall, then. (*Aside.*) He'll finish me if I don't. (*Aloud.*)

> " Mary had a little lamb,
>   Its fleece was white as snow,
> And everywhere that Mary went
>   The lamb was sure to go."

Senator Flurry—Excellent! Go on! Do go on!

Deacon Green—(*Aside*)—He's doubling up his fists! (*Aloud.*)

> " It followed her to school one day,
>   Which was against the rule,
> And made the scholars laugh and play,
>   To see a lamb at school."

I don't know no more. 'Pon my word, I don't, Mr. Fuzzy; I don't, as a good deacon.

Senator Flurry—Ha, ha! This is too good! How capitally you hit off those whining deacons. I detest them, and I always want to have a round with them!

Deacon Green—(*Aside*)—He's gettin' savage! Oh, dear! (*Aloud.*)—So do I, squire; So do I! But, oh lor! I'd like to see the man who would talk agin rings. I'd have his life on the spot.

Senator Flurry—(*Aside.*)—Bless me, I'm getting

shaky! What did Stone say would pacify him? I know. (*Aloud.*) Now, my dear Roscius, you must gratify me with a reading.

DEACON GREEN—Oh, but squire—

SENATOR FLURRY—Nothing but a reading will satisfy me. I'm getting excited to hear you read.

DEACON GREEN—(*Aside*)—Ned said he was bloodthirsty when excited. (*Aloud.*) Wall, I can't disoblige ye. (*Takes up paper.*) Here's a good thing, I guess. (*Reads.*) "Gentlemen of this honorable body, I rise to denounce a villain who rears his head amongst us—"

SENATOR FLURRY—(*Aside*)—Why, that's Bombast's speech. (*Aloud.*) Stop! my dear sir, stop!

DEACON GREEN—(*Aside*)—Ned said to keep on, and not give him a chance.

SENATOR FLURRY—(*Aside*)—I must near him at all risks. (*Edges toward* DEACON GREEN, *who edges away.*)

DEACON GREEN—"He pretends that in purchasing a new site and erecting a new light-house, instead of buying his worthless property, that we do the State an injury. Gentlemen, what are his motives?—"

SENATOR FLURRY—Stop! I wont hear any more! (*Aside.*) He's getting wild! His blood is up!

DEACON GREEN—"Gentlemen, those motives are personal profit; personal gratification; personal meanness! He wishes us to take his old barn for a light-house and to erect a tower from the hay-loft—"

SENATOR FLURRY—Stop! stop!

DEACON GREEN—"And yet this monster has dared to accuse us of corrupt principles, of f-r-a-u-d-fraudulent proceedings, in regard to the Light-house Bill."

SENATOR FLURRY—(*Aside*)—What shall I do to quiet him? (*Pulls his lip.*)

DEACON GREEN—(*Aside*)—Jerusha! There's his lip

a-comin' down. I feel his fist already. I'll try Ned's remedy. (*Grabs his ear.*)

SENATOR FLURRY—(*Aside*)—He's violent; I'll try Stone's remedy. (*Pulls his nose.*)

DEACON GREEN—Oh, Mr. Fusty, don't, please don't! (*Grabs a chair.*)

SENATOR FLURRY—Let go my ear, Roscius, do! (*Does the same.*)

DEACON GREEN—Don't you strike me, then, Prize-fighter.

SENATOR FLURRY—Prize-fighter? What do you call a member of the legislature a prize-fighter for, Roscius?

DEACON GREEN—My name aint Roscius.

SENATOR FLURRY—I'm not a prize-fighter.

DEACON GREEN—Ned told me so.

SENATOR FLURRY—He said your name was Roscius.

DEACON GREEN—I'm Deacon Zachariah Green of Squash Hollow.

SENATOR FLURRY—And I'm Xenophon Flurry, Senator.

DEACON GREEN—Squire, I reckon I'm sold.

SENATOR FLURRY—And so am I; by Ned Stone.

[*Exit* NED.

DEACON GREEN—He said ye was a lion.

SENATOR FLURRY—He represented you as one.

DEACON GREEN—Let's go and pay him up. I'm ready if ye be, if I am a deacon.

SENATOR FLURRY—So we will.

DEACON GREEN—Jerushy but ye scared me!

SENATOR FLURRY—I never lost my equanimity. But come, let us show him that we still are—

BOTH—A PAIR OF LIONS.

[*Curtain.*]

THE CONJUGATING GERMAN.

CHARACTERS:—JOHN, an Englishman.
JONATHAN, an American.
GOTTLIEB, a grave looking German.

SCENE I.—A restaurant. JOHN and JONATHAN seated together at one end of a table and GOTTLIEB at the other.

JOHN—(*To* JONATHAN)—Sir, did you hear of that celebrated dwarf that has arrived in the city?

GOTTLIEB—(*Before* JONATHAN *has time to answer*)—I arrive, thou arrivest, he arrives; we arrive, you arrive, they arrive.

JOHN—(*Looking around at* GOTTLIEB *in surprise*)—Did you speak to me, sir?

GOTTLIEB—I speak, thou speakest, he speaks; we speak, you speak, they speak.

JOHN—(*Angrily*)—How is this? Do you mean to insult me?

GOTTLIEB—I insult, thou insultest, he insults; we insult, you insult, they insult.

JOHN—(*Still more angrily*)—This is too much! I will have satisfaction! If you have any spirit with your rudeness come along with me.

GOTTLIEB—(*Arising and following* JOHN *without any resistance; while* JONATHAN *in the rear looks on with surprise and interest*)—I come, thou comest, he comes; we come, you come, they come.

[*Curtain.*]

SCENE II.—An alley.

JOHN—(*Flourishing a loaded cane threateningly*)—Now sir, you must fight me!

GOTTLIEB—(*Coolly disarming his antagonist*)—I fight, thou fightest, he fights; we fight, you fight, they fight.

John—(*In a milder tone*)—Well, you have the best of it, and I hope you are satisfied.

Gottlieb—I am satisfied, thou art satisfied, he is satisfied; we are satisfied, you are satisfied, they are satisfied.

John—I am glad everybody is satisfied. But pray, leave off quizzing me in this strange manner; and tell me what your object, if you have any, is in doing so?

Gottlieb—I am a German; and am learning the English language. I find it very difficult to remember the peculiarities of the verbs; and my tutor has advised me, in order to fix them in my mind, to conjugate every English verb that I hear spoken. This I have made it a rule to do. I don't like to have my plans broken in upon, while they are in operation, or I would have told you of this before.

Jonathan—(*Laughing heartily*)—Really, gentlemen, this is a pleasant ending to what, a few minutes ago, threatened to be a very unpleasant affair; and we see, herein exemplified, two prominent national traits of character, namely, German perseverance, and an Englishman's determination to obtain satisfaction for insulted dignity, whether personal or national. Come! Let us go back into the restaurant now, and dine together.

Gottlieb—(*As the three retire from the stage*)—I will dine, thou wilt dine, he will dine; we will dine, you will dine, they will dine.

Jonathan—And we'll all dine together.

[*Curtain.*]

Note.—Gottlieb's portion of the above may be Germanized, if deemed expedient.

WHERE THERE'S A WILL THERE'S A WAY.

A DRAMATIC PROVERB.

CHARACTERS:—Mr. Lancey.
Mrs. Lancey.
Mary, their Daughter.

Scene.—A parlor. Mary and her mother sewing. Mr. Lancey pacing the floor and making extravagant gestures.

Mr. Lancey—It is a vile weed, poisons the blood, renders me obnoxious to my wife and children; I will use no more of it. (*Throws something out of the window.*)

Mrs. Lancey—Edward, what is it you are throwing away?

Mr. Lancey—My tobacco! Was it not well done?

Mrs. Lancey—(*Aside to* Mary)—Go secretly and get it, he will want it again. [*Exit* Mary.

Mr. Lancey—(*Gesticulating*)—Never shall that sweet daughter look at me with reproach in her face. Never shall my patient wife upbraid me. Now at last I am "unashamed of soul." Mary, where are my spectacles?

Enter Mary.

Mary—(*Placing tobacco on the shelf*)—Here, papa. (*Giving him spectacles.*) I found them in a pan of milk. But, indeed, you need not have thrown away your tobacco.

Mr. Lancey—Say not a word! Do I not know your prejudices? "To a father waxing old, nothing is dearer than a daughter." It pleases me to do this, nay, I would gladly do more for my little Mary. Ah, wife, what a comfort our children have been to us! Do you remember the first year we were married, how we lived in that yellow house at Nantucket, and ate our meals from that little round table, with only the cat for company?

Mrs. Lancey—Ah, yes, Edward.

Mr. Lancey—Not a chick or child in the house. Do you remember it, Mary?

Mary—Father, you forget, I was not born then. Indeed I never saw Nantucket, and the two older ones have never been there.

Mr. Lancey—Yes, yes, child; what a dunce I am. I sometimes think I am like poor George the Third, who would have been a wise man if his brains had done him any good. (*Puts hand to his head.*)

Mrs. Lancey—Dear Edward, how is your head this morning?

Mr. Lancey—It's a whirligig, it's a top, it's a double and twisted locomotive. (*Walks to right and left.*) It may seem very foolish to ask such a question; but if you will be so kind as to show me which is the hall door, I shall be greatly obliged. Time was when I knew that door like my A B C's. (*Wife goes out with him.*)

Mrs. Lancey—(*Returning*)—Dear, afflicted man; I fear he grows rapidly worse.

Mary—But, mother, there may be hope; let us not despair.

Mrs. Lancey—There is no hope, Mary, in such a case as your father's. Softening of the brain has already commenced.

Mary—It is very, very sad. But, mother, is it not consoling to reflect that this dreadful calamity has not been caused by intemperance?

Mrs. Lancey—You are a sweet comforter, my child. If the present is ever so dark, you turn it around till you find a bright spot on it.

(*Bell rings, and* Mary *goes to the door.*)

Mary—(*Returning*)—Here is a bill from the firm of Comstock & Co. Let us see what it can be.

(*Opens and reads:*)

Dr.	For 7 horse-shoes,	$ 2.50.
	" 5 prs. andirons,	10.00.
	" 1 bbl. shoe-pegs,	3.00.

O mother, mother.

For 1 Cant Dog Beam—

Now pray tell me what can that be?

Mrs. Lancey—O Mary, I do not know; I have heard the term, "cant dog beam" used by lumbermen, and so I presume, in his dazed way, your poor father has been dreaming he is going to drive logs.

Mary—And make shoes, too, mother, or why did he buy a barrel of pegs? And he intends to be a blacksmith at the same time, hence his seven horse-shoes. Poor dear papa.

Mrs. Lancey—And here we have barely money enough for your next music bill, and the new dress which you so sorely need. Mary, what shall we do?

Mary—Wait, mamma, I have it. The drayman is even now at the back yard with his preposterous load of shoe-pegs, andirons and horse-shoes; I will run and tell him to carry them all back again. He surely will not refuse.

Mrs. Lancey—Do so, my child. Tell him your father is not accountable for his purchases. We must persuade Mr. Comstock not to trust him again. [*Exit* Mary.

Enter Mr. Lancey.

Mr. Lancey—I can't find it. (*With excitement.*) Can't find it. Have been searching these premises like a lynx-eyed constable, and I tell you it's gone—vanished—taken to itself wings. My kingdom for a fig.

Mrs. Lancey—My good husband, compose yourself. What is it you have lost?

Mr. Lancey—A pocket full of tobacco. I had it this morning, but now it's gone. "Tobacco gone, all's gone. Better never have been born!"

Mrs. Lancey—(*Aside*)—Poor man. Who with a heart would deny him the paltry comfort of such a thing as this? (*Gives him the paper of tobacco from the shelf.*) There, put it away, dear, and don't lose it again.

Mr. Lancey—(*Putting it in a silver case.*) Thank you, Emily, with all my heart. Your unwearied kindness reminds me—reminds me—of a proverb, but I declare I can't think what it is. Perhaps it's this: "An egg to-day is better than a hen to-morrow."

Mrs. Lancey—(*Smiling*)—A good proverb, Edward; but not particularly to the point.

Enter Mary.

Mary—(*Breathless, with bonnet on*)—O mother, I couldn't make the drayman stop. He insisted upon unloading those ridiculous barrels. So there was nothing I could do but go round to Mr. Comstock's myself, and try to reason with him.

Mrs. Lancey—I hope he relented.

Mary—No indeed, mamma. He said a bargain was a bargain, and if my father had bought a cart load of street mud, it would be—

Mrs. Lancey—Scarcely more absurd.

Mr. Lancey—Why, wife, why Mary, who has been buying trumpery? Not I.

Mrs. Lancey—(*Kindly*)—Some articles you have sent home, dear, will be of no use in our family. We can not eat pegs, and we have no horses to be shod. Try and remember next time not to make any purchases at all. You say your head whirls very unpleasantly, and Mary and I ought to spare you the trouble of providing for the family.

Mr. Lancey—Now, Emily, I can not consent to burden you so much. It is not only my duty, it is a positive pleasure to me to occupy my mind with planning pleasant little suprises for you and Mary.

(*Fumbles for door; assisted by* Mrs. Lancey, *goes out.*)

Mrs. Lancey—(*Sighing*)—Pleasant surprises. Mary, what shall we do? This bill is a heavy one.

Mary—Mamma, I've been thinking, and as one plan has failed us, we must try another. If Mr. Comstock will insist upon being paid, why, I can go without my new dress.

Mrs. Lancey—Bless my dear girl.

(*Bell rings,* Mary *goes to door.*)

Mary—(*Returning, with another bill*)—This is for rides. Dear papa, he must have recreation.

Mrs. Lancey—(*Holding up her hands*)—Fortunately he never thinks of driving a horse himself, otherwise I should live in continual fear. But, Mary, how much is this bill?

Mary—It is twenty-five dollars, and mother, I have already decided that I will give up my next quarter's music. It is, after all, a small sacrifice to make to such a father (*sighs*) as mine was once.

Mrs. Lancey—My heart aches at the thought of it; but really if you can consent to it, I suppose it must be done. I see no alternative.

Enter Mr. Lancey.

Mr. Lancey—(*With old ragged stuffed chair upon his back*)—Here, Emily, is a pleasant surprise.

Mrs. Lancey—(*Looking aghast*)—Why, Edward, what now?

Mr. Lancey—(*Throwing himself panting upon the*

lounge)—I brought it all the way on my back. I thought, in the words of the poet, "My strength is as the strength of ten, because my heart is pure." Still it has fatigued me, you see.

Mrs. Lancey—Then why bring it at all, my love? I'm sure there's no place in the house for it, and the lumber room is full!

Mr. Lancey—Lumber room, indeed! Why, Emily, this chair is a hundred years old.

Mrs. Lancey—I can easily believe it.

Mr. Lancey—(*Panting*)—I bought it at auction, and I assure you I had to bid pretty high.

Mrs. Lancey—I am surprised! Who could have bid against you for such a hideous ruin as—

Mary—(*Aside*)—Be careful, mother, you will wound his feelings.

Mr. Lancey—Who bid against me? Why the relatives of the family, to be sure. You must know, Emily, this is a precious heirloom.

Mary—(*Laughing, and turning it over and looking at the bottom of it*)—It is called a loom, perhaps, because it's covered with webs—cobwebs.

Mrs. Lancey—But, Edward, who were the family relatives, and where was the auction?

Mr. Lancey—The family relatives were the Pickards, the Jewetts, and the—the—I forget the names. And the auction was at—at—

Mary—The widow Pickard's, I presume. I noticed a red flag as I passed the house just now.

Mrs. Lancey—(*Smiling*)—Well, then, this is an heirloom to me, too. Mrs. Pickard, you know, is my cousin. I belong to a branch of the family.

Mary—Delightful! So you do! It is not so bad, after all.

Mr. Lancey—Your mother is pleased. I knew she would be. But here is the bill for the chair.

(*Gives it to* Mrs. Lancey, *and exit.*)

Mrs. Lancey—(*Reads*)—Thirty dollars! O Mary, Mary, I am afraid we shall be obliged to put your poor papa in a Lunatic Asylum. You are fertile in inventions; now tell me what we can do in such a dilemma? Where can we raise money to pay for this article, which nobody wants?

Mary—Dear mother, I can't think just yet; though no doubt the idea will occur to me all in good time. Meanwhile, since we feel disturbed in mind, and can not sit down quietly to our sewing, suppose we employ ourselves in covering this precious heir-loom with patch? It will be a capital lounging-chair, after all, for father.

Mrs. Lancey—But where is the patch to come from, little sunbeam? (*Smiles.*)

Mary—Don't you remember the drab and blue? It's in the clothes-press, I will bring it.

Mrs. Lancey—Not now, dear. Bring the claw-hammer. We will first remove this ragged velvet.

[*Exit* Mary.

Enter Mary.

Mary—Here is the hammer. (*Examines chair.*) Why, mother, what is this? There's a hole here as big as a bird's nest! (*Puts in her hand.*) And here, away down under the horse-hair, is a quantity of paper.

Mrs. Lancey—Take it out carefully. It is probably some old newspaper, and its ancient appearance will be interesting.

Mary—(*Taking out yellow paper*)—This is not a newspaper; it is more like parchment. It has a blue seal and a coat of arms. (*Reads:*) "I, Joshua Boardman, being of sound mind, and—"

Mrs. Lancey—Why, Mary, Mary Lancey, that is a will! Give it to me. (*Takes it eagerly. Reads:*) "Do give and bequeath—" Mary, this is the true will, the lost will of your great-grandfather Boardman.

(*Sits down, wrings her hands.*)

Mary—Well, mother, why don't you speak? Why don't you read it?

Mrs. Lancey—I am overwhelmed, my child. This gives to the heirs of James Boardman,—*James*, do you observe?—all right and title to the estate, worth—why, Mary, it's worth now *one hundred thousand.* It is the—I can't recover my breath, this is so startling—the estate unlawfully possessed by the Jewetts. It's—

Mary—I'm befogged. *You* are an heir of James Boardman?

Mrs. Lancey—Yes, sole surviving heir! This estate, Mary, is mine beyond question. This will was secreted years ago. I have heard there was a search made for it in the days of my ancestors. Now, by what we call an accident, it has come to light.

Mary—Murder will out, and so will a will. Now, mother, we can pay for the chair. I told you an idea would come into my head. I knew there would be some plan by which we could raise the money.

Mrs. Lancey—I hoped there might be; but, my dear girl, I did not dream it would be exactly in this way. Let us be thankful for our great and unexpected blessing.

Mary—Dear mamma, I see now the means of settling all our difficulties, both present and future. Every thing looks bright. I am reminded of the hackneyed proverb—

Mrs. Lancey—Please don't say what it is. Let the *audience* find it out, if they can. (*Both bow.*)

[*Curtain.*]

OTHER PEOPLE'S CHILDREN.

CHARACTERS:—Mrs. Brown, ⎫
Mrs. Green, ⎬ Neighbors.
Mrs. Jones, ⎭
Howard, Mrs. Green's son.
William Henry, Mrs. Brown's son.

SCENE.—A street in a country village, in front of MRS. GREEN's residence; MRS. GREEN sweeping front porch, accosted by MRS. BROWN.

MRS. BROWN—I say, Mrs. Green, if you want peace with the world, and all besides, you may just commence this very day, keeping your children at home, for I can not, and *will* not be bothered with them any longer.

MRS. GREEN—Keep my children at home? Why, Mrs. Brown, you surprise me! I think I should be committing a sin, if I should deprive my children the benefit of our schools and our religious services on the Sabbath. My friend, I am at a loss to know what you mean.

MRS. BROWN—(*Aside*)—I am no friend of hers. (*To* MRS. GREEN.) Only yesterday, one of my—

MRS. GREEN—I am still puzzled to know what you mean! Perhaps the quickest and best way to approach the subject, will be to ask you to explain yourself, for I am growing very impatient.

MRS. BROWN—If you had been *half* as patient as I know I have been, you would have known ere this. As I was going to say: only yesterday my second boy, William Henry, came as straight into the house as he could come, and told me your boy made a continual face at him all the time he was passing the house. If it had been the *first* time, or I knew it would have been the *last*, I'd have just let it pass by without mentioning it.

MRS. GREEN—If Howard has done such a thing as you speak of, he shall be severely reprimanded for it. I hear him now in the back yard, and will call him. Howard! Howard! (*Speaking louder the last time.*)

Howard—(*Behind the curtain*)—What is wanting, mother?

Enter Howard.

Mrs. Green—Mrs. Brown and I are having a little difficulty here, and as you seem to be the main cause of it, I thought it best to speak to you, and correct you for a very great fault that I hear you have committed.

Howard—*Me*, mother?

Mrs. Brown—Innocence, oh, innocence! (*Putting on a dreadful frown.*)

Mrs. Green—Yes, Mrs. Brown tells me you have been making faces at her little boy, which I think to be very wrong.

Howard—Why, mother, I can not think when I did such a thing.

Mrs. Brown—Yesterday!

Mrs. Green—(*At the same time*)—She says you did it yesterday.

Howard—I can not remember it.

Enter William Henry, *walking by, with a slouched hat on, and both pockets full of apples that he is trying to hide.*

Mrs. Brown—William Henry, dear, just wait a minute. Didn't you tell me that Howard Green made a face at you yesterday?

William Henry—Yes I jist did, and I'm going to flax him for it, yit.

Mrs. Brown—(*Addressing* Howard)—Now, my young man, you have two things to answer for. First, making faces at my boy; and second, telling a plain—try-to-get-out-of-it.

Howard—I am going to confess all that I am guilty of. William Henry, what time yesterday did you see me?

William Henry—Jist after breakfast, while the first bell was ringing for school.

Howard—(*Laughing*)—I can now explain the whole thing. Don't you remember, mother, how my tooth had been aching all the morning, and I had just consented to have it drawn as the first school-bell commenced ringing?

Mrs. Green—I do now, indeed.

Howard—I think now it is a plain case, without much further argument. I was going by your house, Mrs. Brown, with hands to my face, suffering very much with my tooth, and hurrying to the dentist's that I might not be too late for school. I guess I must have looked very ridiculous to William Henry, and am willing to confess that I gave him reasons for thinking as he did, though I was innocent of it at the time.

Mrs. Brown—Well, we will let that pass this time, but what I wish to speak most particular about, is this: Now, my children are *good* children, and never interfere in the least with that which does not belong to them; yet I hear a continual complaint about rubber balls being missed, and plates of apples being taken. I mean the apples and not the plates; for I consider the apples alone, a great theft. Now, I don't want a street quarrel here, but William Henry thinks your children are the cause of all complaint.

Mrs. Green—Never make an assertion, Mrs. Brown, unless you have positive proof for it.

Mrs. Brown—(*Very loud*)—Positive proof! I can give—

Enter Mrs. Jones, *hurriedly*.

Mrs. Jones—Good morning, Mrs. Green. Why, Mrs. Brown, I was just going to call upon you about a little matter; but finding you here, it will save me the trouble of going any farther. You seem to have some business on hand already.

Mrs. Brown—Yes, I am a business person, and like to settle things in a business manner. Give in your account, and I will square it off.

Mrs. Jones—Indeed I will, in a very few words. I saw your second son, William Henry, just emptying a plate of apples that were on the table in my front room, and hurry off so fast that I could not speak to him, and I thought it best to call upon you about the matter, and say to you that he has *repeatedly* done the same thing.

Mrs. Brown—Have you "positive proof" of it, as Mrs. Green says?

Mrs. Jones—I *think* I have, if my own eyes don't deceive me.

William Henry—Let's go home, mother, for it's dinner time. (*Starting, and letting an apple fall.*)

Mrs. Green—Wait a moment, William; I think *positive* proof is becoming *visible* proof. Was not that an apple you let fall just now?

William Henry—Y-e-s, m-a-a-m.

Mrs. Green—(*Laughing*)—I think we had better end this very unpleasant difficulty at Mrs. Jones' expense yet; for I remember the Golden Rule, "Do good for evil." I propose that Mrs. Brown's little boy gives each of us an apple, and returns the rest to the rightful owner, keeping none for himself; which may afterwards jog his memory should he ever think of stealing apples again.

Mrs. Jones—I consent.

Howard—So do I.

[William Henry *sheepishly takes the apples from his pockets, and distributes them.*]

[*Curtain.*]

GOOD MAXIMS.

CHARACTERS:—First, a Boy or Girl.
Second, a Class, to represent Audience.

First—Pardon a friend who ventures to give
A few simple rules to assist you to live.

Second—Go on! Go on!

First—" Early to bed, and early to rise,
Will make a man healthy and wealthy and wise."

Second—Good! Good! That's true! (*Applause.*)

First—Better be late than never to come,
But better, a great deal, be just on the time.

Second—Good! Very true!

First—Better be poor, and have a good name,
Than wicked, and wealthy, and blazoned with fame.

Second—That's true! (*Triple applause.*)

First—Pray tell me, dear friends, if any one can,
The habits and ways of a nice gentleman?

Second—Please tell us.

First—This is the rule, and it never fails,
He washes and brushes and pares off his nails.

Second—Good! Good! All right! (*Applause.*)

First—He never profanes the name of the Lord,
Is gentle and loving, and true to his word.

Second—Good! That's true.

First—He never sips rum, or shuffles a card,
Or poisons his breath with the nauseous weed.

Second—Good! Good! All right!

(*Triple applause.*)

First—Is never unkind to parent or wife;
But faithful and true to the end of his life.

Second—All true! That's all true!

[*Curtain.*]

Note.—This may be performed with good effect to fill up the time while preparing for some longer exercise.

THE FLORAL GUIDE.

A HUMOROUS TABLEAU.

There is nothing nicer for an Exhibition, or other like occasion, than a good tableau or two. The following has the merit of simplicity at least, and can be made very amusing by proper preparation.

To be appreciated, the flower or vegetable must be announced quite plainly by the manager, and acted very slowly.

Characters :—In almost every company of young people can be found a "Rose" and a "Lily." "Bouncing Bet" can be represented by a big, hearty Elizabeth, or a smaller person of same name, jumping; "Poppy" by a happy papa, holding a child in his arms; "Lady Slippers" by showing a pair of those useful articles; "Johnny Jump Up" by some John rising suddenly from his chair; "Rocket" by a little girl rocking a cradle; "Morning Glory" by a sleepy boy, without a coat or shoes, with frowsy hair, rubbing his half-opened eyes; "Pink" by a foppish young man, daintily strutting, with beaver, kids and cane; "Tulips" by two pair of lips in greeting, and "Sweet Williams" by two boys of that name.

In the "Vegetable Department" a small boy is poised on his head, held in place by a larger one, for "Turnip;" another small boy *strikes* the first one for "Beets;" while the "big boy" pushes both over, for "Squash," and a fourth boy takes handkerchief from last boy's pocket for "Cabbage." (*Each action to be separately named.*) Tom standing with eight capital O's pinned to his coat is "Tom-a-toes;" some one displaying auburn hair is "Radish" (red-dish); and a boy plucking flower from girl's hair is "Caul-i-flower" (cull-I-flower). This whole display will occupy but a few minutes, and if desirable, may be prolonged by anything a fertile fancy may suggest.

[*Curtain.*]

THE THREE WISHES.

CHARACTERS:—QUEEN OF THE FAIRIES.
FIRST FAIRY, the Fairy of Truth.
SECOND FAIRY, the Fairy of Love.
THIRD FAIRY, the Fairy Youth.
Other Fairies.
FIRST GIRL.
SECOND GIRL.
BOY.

SCENE.—A group of Fairies with hands joined. (They sing or speak.)

A thousand years ago we met,
  Around this aged tree,
And yet, though years have rolled away,
  A youthful band are we.
And yet, though years have rolled away,
  We sing our songs with glee.

QUEEN—What have you done this thousand years?
FIRST FAIRY—I've wiped away unnumbered tears.
SECOND FAIRY—I've quieted unnumbered fears.
THIRD FAIRY—How did you do it? I could not,
Though I'm the bright fairy of Youth,
I could not cleanse them of one dark blot.
Tell me, O fairy of Truth.
FIRST FAIRY—I showed them the Truth, and I strove hard to win
Their hearts from the dangerous inroads of sin.
THIRD FAIRY—And now tell me how, O fairy of Love,
Men's hearts from the pleasures of earth you could move?
SECOND FAIRY—Whene'er I knew their hearts to rove,
I chained them to the Throne Above;
To those I knew that knew not God,
I showed their Saviour's pard'ning blood.
QUEEN—Come, let us go to earth again,
    Visit together the children of men,
    See which will win—
    Heaven or Sin,
    Truth or Beauty,
    Youth or Duty.

Enter FIRST *and* SECOND GIRL, *and* BOY. (*They should act as if they did not see the fairies, who should all face them. The children should seat themselves on the floor.*)

FIRST GIRL—I wonder if the story of Cinderella is true.
BOY—Why, Sis, you never see fairies *now*.
SECOND GIRL—No, *we* do n't, but maybe other people do.
BOY—Well, if there are any, I'd like to see one—just once. (QUEEN *nods gently.*)
FIRST GIRL—Look at that Lily. Did n't it nod beautifully?

Second Girl—So strangely, too.

(*Fairies all nod to each other, and to the children.*)

Boy—They all seem nodding—Oh, *so* strangely.

First Girl—It almost seems as if fairies were here.

(*Fairies all step forward. Children are frightened.*)

Queen—We are here,
    Children dear.
    What will you have,
    For we will give,
    What you may ask?

All the Fairies—A pleasant task.

Queen—Be not afraid to speak.

Second Girl—Give to me beauty. Make me amiable. Give me wealth and a long life, full of pleasure.

Queen—These we grant to thee.

First Fairy—Yet to me thy wishes are
    Vain as searches for the star
    That goes from sight, in darkest night,
    A bright but—*dying* meteor!

Boy—Give me strength, and with it energy, a strong mind and a strong body. And give to me, too, a brave, open heart. Make me a *man*.

Queen—Thy wish is granted thee.

First Fairy—Indeed, right joyfully,
    Thy wish is granted thee.
    And yet methinks I see
    Something that thou dost lack.
    Oh, mayest thou not, as I believe,
    Ever look mournful back
    O'er the gifts thou didst receive.

First Girl—Fairy, I don't know for what to ask. Beauty must fade, and I would not be always young. Give me *Love*—Love to God, and to my fellows everywhere.

Queen—With thee, daughter, we agree.
　　All things added unto thee,
　　From the God who loves, shall be.
Second Fairy—Lord, I thank thee, thou hast brought
　　　To her mind this holy thought.
　　　Bless it, bless it! While she basks
　　　In thy Love-light, what she asks,
　　　And more, be given unto her.
　　　(*Fairies join hands, and look upward.*)
　　With the Love
　　From Thee above,
　　Give them *Truth*
　　To guide their youth!
Give them true beauty of life and heart;
Keep them afar from sin apart;
　　Guide them, and keep them,
　　　Safe from harm;
　　Helpless lambkins,
　　　Under Thine arm.
　　　[*Curtain.*]

TURN ABOUT'S FAIR PLAY.

CHARACTERS:—Mr. Fairbairn.
　　　　　　Mrs. Fairbairn.
　　　　　　Tom,　⎱ their Children.
　　　　　　Kitty,⎰
　　　　　　Aunt Betsey, a maiden Aunt.

Scene I.—Parlor. Late in the afternoon, or evening.

Tom—(*Spitefully kicking the ottoman*)—"You can't do this," and "you mustn't do that," from morning to night.

Enter Kitty.

Kitty—(*With a frown*)—What were you saying? I hope you don't feel as cross as I do.

Tom—Cross is no word for it. It's so terribly warm. (*Fanning himself with his hat.*) And I wanted to go to the river to cool off. And papa told me to take a book and sit still. Just as if that could keep me cool. But what is the matter with you? I declare you don't *look* any more amiable than I *feel*.

Kitty—Amiable is no word for it. Mamma has made me dress up in this stiff, clean frock, and have my hair combed again, because she says some one *may* come. I want to play in the garden, and I can't when I'm all fussed up in this way, with ruffles, and bows, and sash. I do hate company, and clothes, and manners, don't you?

Tom—Yes, I do. I hate being ordered round everlastingly from morning till night. I'd just like to be let alone. Well, if we can't have a game of romps, let us go down to the gate and see other children have a nice time.

Enter Mr. *and* Mrs. Fairbairn *and sit down. The former tips back in a chair with his paper, the latter takes up her embroidery.* Aunt Betsey *comes in knitting, with glasses and big apron on.*

Mrs. Fairbairn—(*Goes to the door*)—Come, children, the dew is falling. You'll take cold.

Enter Tom *and* Kitty *pouting, and take seats.*

Mrs. Fairbairn—I believe this warm weather affects the health of the children. They look pale and languid. They need something bracing. I shall give them a dose of iron mixture in the morning.

Kitty—Oh, my! (*Making up a face.*) I've taken enough now to make a cooking stove.

Tom—I'd feel all right if I could go swimming every night. Aunt Betsey used to let the nephews who lived with her go.

Mr. Fairbairn—(*Sharply*)—Aunt Betsey's ideas and

mine differ. Children are not brought up now as they were in her day.

Tom—I wish they were. Jolly good times her nephews used to have. Papa, she has told me about it; and how you used to play with them.

[MR. FAIRBAIRN *lays down his paper.* MRS. FAIRBAIRN *looks up interested.*]

KITTY—Yes! And her nieces used to have good times, too, when they came to the farm. They used to play everything they liked. And were not afraid of soiling their clothes; for they did not have to be rigged up, and plagued with company every day.

MR. FAIRBAIRN—What do you mean by that?

TOM—If *you* were to be in our places for a day, you'd *see* what we mean.

AUNT BETSEY—(*Smiling*)—Wouldn't it be worth your while to try the experiment?

(MR. FAIRBAIRN *and* MRS. FAIRBAIRN *laugh.*)

AUNT BETSEY—(*Earnestly*)—Why not put yourselves in their places for a day, and see how you like it? I think you would understand the case better than any one could describe it; and, perhaps, do both yourselves and the children a lasting service.

MR. FAIRBAIRN—(*Much amused*)—Upon my word, that's a droll idea! What do you say to it, mamma?

MRS. FAIRBAIRN—I am willing to try if you are, just for the fun of the thing; but I don't think it will do any good. (*Children clap their hands.*)

MR. FAIRBAIRN—How do you propose to carry out this new educational frolic? (*Looking a bit worried.*)

AUNT BETSEY—Merely let the children do as they like for one day, and have full power over you. Let them plan your duties and pleasures, order your food, fix your hours and punish or reward you as they think proper. You must promise entire obedience, and keep the agreement till night.

TOM and KITTY—Good! good! Oh, wont it be fun?

AUNT BETSEY—As to-morrow is a holiday for us all, let us celebrate it by this funny experiment. It will amuse us, and do no harm at any rate.

MR. FAIRBAIRN—Very well, we will. Come, mamma, let us promise, and see what these rogues will do for us. Playing father and mother is no joke, mind you; but *you* will have an easier time of it than *we* do, for *we shall behave ourselves.*

[*Curtain.*]

SCENE II.—Next day. Morning. KITTY enters the room with a long dress, and the airs of a grown-up person, looks annoyed as she picks up books and balls, saying, "What careless children! How I wish they would learn to be orderly!" Busies herself with AUNT BETSEY setting the breakfast table. MRS. FAIRBAIRN enters with loose hair, and light cool wrapper.

KITTY—(*Solemnly*)—Careless, untidy girl. Put on a clean dress, do up your hair properly, and then practice this new music until breakfast.

[MRS. FAIRBAIRN *hesitates, looks as if she would rather not, then goes out.*]

Enter TOM, *with long coat, neck-tie, beaver hat, cane, etc.*

TOM—Good morning, Mrs. Fairbairn. Good morning, Betsey Jane. Why, where's that boy? Hasn't he got up yet? (*Calls at the door:*) Get up, get up! (*A voice whines out:*) "Come,—you-let-me-alone. It-is n't-time-yet."

TOM—(*Solemnly*)—No, no! lazy-bones, get up. (*Takes out his watch.*) There, you have been called; and now if you are not down in fifteen minutes, you wont have any breakfast. Not a morsel, sir; not a morsel.

[*Breakfast bell rings.* MRS. FAIRBAIRN *comes in hurriedly in a stiff calico, with braided hair, and white apron.*]

Kitty—Go back and enter the room properly. Will you never learn to behave like a lady?

Mrs. Fairbairn—(*Looks impatient, but obeys, passes her plate*)—Some biscuit, and trout, if you please.

Kitty—No fish, or hot bread for you, my dear. Eat your good oat-meal porridge and milk; that is the proper food for children.

Mrs. Fairbairn—Can't I have some coffee?

Kitty—(*Pouring out and sipping a large cup of her own*)—Certainly not. *I* never was allowed coffee when a little girl, and couldn't think of giving it to *you*.

Mrs. Fairbairn—Oh, dear!

[Mrs. Fairbairn *eats porridge with a wry face.* Tom *sits in an arm-chair, reads paper, and eats heartily.* Aunt Betsey *looks pleased.*]

Enter Mr. Fairbairn.

Tom—(*Looks at watch*)—What did I tell you, sir? You are late again, sir. No breakfast, sir. I'm sorry, but this habit *must* be broken up. Not a word; it's your own fault, and you must bear the penalty.

Mr. Fairbairn—Come, now, that's hard on a fellow! I'm awful hungry. Can't I have just a bite of something? (*Stepping towards table.*)

Tom—(*Rises and stamps his foot*)—I said—not—a—morsel! And I shall keep my word. Go to your morning duties, and let this be a lesson to you.

[*They rise from the table, and all leave the room but* Mr. Fairbairn. *He sits biting the end off his cigar, which he has found, after much rummaging in his pockets.* Aunt Betsey *comes in, on tip-toe, and slips a biscuit and a cookie in his hand.*]

Aunt Betsey—My dear, do try and please your father. He is right. But—I can't bear to see you starve.

Mr. Fairbairn—(*With mouth full*)—Betsey, you are an angel. (*Eating very fast.*) Do you think these rogues will keep it up in this rigorous style all day?

Aunt Betsey—I trust so; it isn't a bit over-done. Hope you like it. (*Goes out laughing.*)

Enter Kitty *and* Mrs. Fairbairn.

Kitty—Now, put on your hat, and draw baby up and down the avenue for an hour. Don't go on the grass, or you will wet your feet. Don't play with the baby; I want her to go to sleep. Don't talk to your brother, or he will neglect his work. His father wants him to rake in the yard.

Mrs. Fairbairn—Must I, really? It's so warm, and I want to sew. Kitty, you are a hard-hearted mamma, to make me do it.

Kitty—*I* have to do it every morning, and *you* don't let me off. (*Getting a bottle.*) Here is your iron mixture, dear. Now, take it, like a good girl.

Mrs. Fairbairn—(*Stepping back*)—*I wont!*

Kitty—Then Aunty will hold your hands, and I shall make you.

Mrs. Fairbairn—But I don't like it; I don't need it.

Kitty—Neither do I, but you give it to me all the same. I'm sure you need strengthening more than I do; you have so many "trials." (Kitty *looks sly.*)

Enter Aunt Betsey.

Aunt Betsey—You'd better mind, Carrie; it can't hurt you, and you know you promised entire obedience.

Mrs. Fairbairn—But I never thought these little chits would do so well. (*Drinking it.*) Ugh, how disagreeable it is!

Kitty—When you come in, sit down, and hem these

towels until dinner time. I declare! I have so much to do, and so many cares, I don't know which way to turn!

[Evening.—TOM and KITTY dressed to go out riding.]

MR. FAIRBAIRN—Can't I go over and see Mr. Hammond?

TOM—No; I don't like Billy Hammond, so I don't wish you to play with his father. (*Smiling.*)

(MR. FAIRBAIRN *gives a long, low whistle.*)

MR. FAIRBAIRN—(*Respectfully*)—Going to drive, sir?

TOM—Don't ask questions.

MRS. FAIRBAIRN—Can't I go?

KITTY—No; there isn't room.

MR. FAIRBAIRN—Why not have the carry-all, and let us go, too; we like it so much. (*In a pleasing tone.*)

TOM—(*Impatiently*)—We can't be troubled with you. The buggy is nicest, and lightest, and we want to talk over our affairs. You, my son, can help John turn the hay in the lawn, and Caroline can amuse the baby, or help Jane with the preserves. Little girls should be domestic.

MR. FAIRBAIRN—Oh! thunder!

KITTY—Aunt Betsey taught you that speech, you saucy boy. (*Shaking her finger at him.*) Now, Caroline, I expect company this evening, but I don't wish you to sit up. You are too young, and late hours are bad for your eyes. Go to bed at seven, and don't forget to brush your hair and teeth well, five minutes for each; cold-cream your hands, fold your ribbons, hang up your clothes, put out your boots to be cleaned, and put in the mosquito-bars. I will come and take away the light, when I return.

[*Exit* MR. *and* MRS. FAIRBAIRN.

TOM—Hasn't it been a funny day?

Kitty—Don't think I quite like it, every thing is so turned around.

Tom—Guess *they* didn't like it very well. I wonder if our joke will do any good.

Aunt Betsey—(*Smiling and knitting, with happy face*)—Wait and see, little dears.

[*Curtain.*]

FRIGHTENED AT NOTHING.

CHARACTERS:—Mrs. Ketchem.
Lillie, an Orphan, her Niece.
Nettie, } School Girls.
Lucy, }
Frank.

Scene I.—A neat room.

Enter Lucy *and* Nettie *talking.*

Nettie—Wont that be grand? But do you think we can do it?

Lucy—I guess so. How lucky it is for us, that she believes in ghosts, spirits, and such things. But I don't believe she ever saw one. Wont she be surprised?

Nettie—Poor Lillie! I feel so sorry for her; she has to stay at home all the time; Mrs. Ketchem wont let her go anywhere; but I thought, perhaps she would let her go to our picnic, when we got it up more on her account than any thing else.

Lucy—Yes, and isn't it too mean, she wont let her go now? But I am determined she *shall* go, if I can do any thing to help her.

Nettie—But do you suppose Lillie will go, if we can get her aunt's consent the way we spoke of?

Lucy—By frightening her into consenting, you mean?

Yes, I think she will, but she would not if her aunt was not so unkind to her.

NETTIE—Hark! I hear somebody coming, let's hide and see who it is. (*They hide behind a table.*)

Enter FRANK.

FRANK—(*Talking to himself*)—I declare it's too bad, I wish her aunt was in Mexico. I wonder if I can't contrive some means to make her aunt let her go—but—

NETTIE—You'll have to get *ghosts* to help you.

FRANK—Ghosts! (*Looking around.*) Who is that?

NETTIE—The shadow of your Aunt Betsy Jane.

FRANK—(*Laughing*)—Why she's alive. Seems to me that voice sounds like Nettie Gay's.

NETTIE—(*Coming out*)—So it is. (*To* LUCY.) Stay there a minute. (*To* FRANK.) And so you too, are wondering how you can get Lillie to attend our picnic?

FRANK—Yes, can't you help me?

LUCY—(*From under the table*)—You'll have to get ghosts to help you.

FRANK—(*Starting*)—Well if there isn't another! I believe the house is haunted. Who are you?

LUCY—The great grandfather of your departed Uncle George.

FRANK—(*Looking under table*)—Come out of there, Lucy, you can't scare me.

LUCY—(*Coming out*)—But perhaps we could scare Mrs. Ketchem.

FRANK—What do you mean?

LUCY—Let's go out in the yard, and we will tell you what a nice plan we have, for making Mrs. Ketchem let Lillie go with us to-morrow. [*Exit.*

[*Curtain.*]

Scene II.—Time evening. Mrs. Ketchem knitting. Lillie washing dishes.

Mrs. Ketchem—You needn't ask me any more. I say *you shan't go.* If you tease me any more, I *vum,* I will box your ears.

Lillie—But, aunt, I haven't been anywhere for the *longest time,* and I will be real good if you will—

Mrs. Ketchem—What did I tell you?

[*Jumps up, dropping her work, runs toward* Lillie, *with her hand raised.* Lillie *dodges around the table. Suddenly a knock at the door.*]

Mrs. Ketchem—Goodness gracious! Who is that? It can't be Hezekiah. Lillie, you just wait 'till I see who this is, then I will 'tend to your case, young lady. You needn't think you are going to get off so.

(*Opens door, shrieks and starts back.*)

Enter Frank *dressed as ghost of* Lillie's *mother.* Lillie, *pretending fright, hides behind chair.*

Frank—(*Solemnly*)—Mrs. Ketchem, sister of my dead husband. Do you treat my child as I commanded you? Speak!

Mrs. Ketchem—(*Gasping*)—Yes. Oh go away, go away!

Frank—Remember I am always watching you. All your actions I see; I know how cruelly you have treated my child, and now I will remain here, until you promise to treat her better than you have done.

Mrs. Ketchem—(*Covering her head with her apron*)—Oh, don't stay, I haven't done—

Frank—Hush! You needn't attempt to deceive me, I know all. Will you promise never more to abuse my daughter Lillie? Will you solemnly promise to treat her hereafter as your own daughter?

Mrs. Ketchem—Yes, I will promise any thing, only go away, go away!

Frank—I will go soon, and will not appear again, unless I find—

Mrs. Ketchem—Oh, do n't come again, I will—I mean I wont box her ears any more. Oh!

Frank—If you don't let her go to the picnic to-morrow, I will appear again, and woe be to you, if I come forth again. Farewell. [*Exit slowly.*

Mrs. Ketchem—Has she gone? Has she gone *sure?* Well; I suppose I will have to let you go to the picnic, after all. (*Knock.*) Hark! is n't somebody knocking? Oh, she has come back, she has come back! Mercy, mercy!

[*Runs frantically around the room, while* Lillie *opens the door, ushering in* Lucy, Nettie *and* Frank.]

Lillie—(*Aside to them*)—She is frightened 'most to death. It is too bad.

Nettie—It is n't either. It's just what she deserves.

Frank—It worked well, did n't it? Did n't I make a capital ghost?

Lillie—Yes indeed, but be careful; she will hear us.

Lucy—(*To* Mrs. Ketchem)—We have come again, to see if we can't coax you to let Lillie go with us to-morrow. Please let her go.

Mrs. Ketchem—I will this time—but next time—

Frank—(*In a sepulchral voice*)—Remember your promise. (*All start—looking around.*)

All—Who was that?

Mrs. Ketchem—(*Nervously*)—It must have been the door creaking. Yes, Lillie may go. Now I suppose you are satisfied.

Frank—Oh, yes, I can answer for all. But I must go now. Come girls; come, Lillie; I have something to tell you. [*Exit* Lillie, Lucy, Nettie *and* Frank.

Mrs. Ketchem—Who would have thought it? But I always did believe in ghosts, now I am sure of it. I believe I *have* treated poor Lillie rather badly. But it is all owing to my rheumatiz, it makes me so cross, but I will try and be easier on her. But what are they talking so long about? I must go tell them to finish their chat to-morrow. It is getting late. [*Exit.*

[*Curtain.*]

"BOARDING 'ROUND."
AN EXPERIENCE OF THE OLDEN TIME.

CHARACTERS:—Miss Landen, Teacher of a country School.
Tom,　} Pupils.
Lily,
Mr. Jenks.
Mrs. Jenks.
Jack,　} their Sons.
Ike,
Sally, their Daughter.

Scene I.—A country school-house—teacher seated at her desk; her head leaning wearily on her hand.

Miss Landen—Ah, well! another day's labor in this dingy old school-room is ended, and now comes the unwelcome question: Where am I to lay my weary head to-night? Where shall I get something to satisfy the cravings of nature, that is fit to eat? How *do* these people subsist on food that would disgust a Camanche Indian! I have been compelled to live on baked beans and pork, buckwheat cakes and "sop," until I abhor and loathe the sight, smell, or thought of them. And, being obliged to sleep in a different house every night, and being obliged to "do the agreeable," no matter how weary or preoccupied, to such uncultivated, vulgar people, who seem to think they are doing a deed of charity, for which

I must be duly grateful, in giving me a night's lodging, and a seat at their table. I declare, it's just like living on the town, and worse—for at the poor-house, one has at least a permanent home. True, for the last week I have had a pleasant stopping-place with Mrs. Sanderson, the only woman in the place that lives like a civilized Christian. But before going there—at my "boarding-house"—there was the alternative of sitting up all night, or sleeping with two of my promising pupils—whom I could hardly endure as near me as the recitation bench, so redolent were they of grease and dirt. If there were a place, within two or three miles, where I could buy provisions, I'd rent a room and set up house-keeping myself. I'd have, perhaps, twenty-five cents a week left.

Enter TOM, LILY, *and* IKE, *pupils.*

TOM—Say, school marm! aint ye goin' to our house to-night? Mother told me to ask ye if it wasn't 'bout time for ye to come ag'in.

MISS LANDEN—(*Aside*)—Nothing there but the everlasting pork and beans, and beds alive with bugs. (*Aloud.*) No, Tom, I guess not to-night, some other time I'll go with you.

LILY—Will you go with me again to-night, Miss Landen? You know mamma is always glad to have you come.

MISS LANDEN—It is a great temptation. I should like so much to go. (*Aside.*) Oh, if I could stop with Mrs. Sanderson all the time, I should be content. (*Aloud.*) But not to-night, dear; I have already stayed with your mother far more than her allotted portion of "boarding the teacher," and I can not further trespass on her hospitality. (*Aside.*) Where shall I go?

IKE JENKS—(*Marching up to the desk, with hands* in

his pockets)—Mother says she's got to have you to board *some time,* and she wants you to be sure and come to-night, 'cause father's been to the "Burg" to-day, and she'd rayther you'd come when she's got tea and sugar in the house.

Miss Landen—(*Aside*)—As well there as anywhere. (*Aloud.*) Yes, I'll go with you! How far do your parents reside from here?

Ike—How fur do they *what?*

Miss Landen—Do you live far from here?

Ike—No, *mawm,* only a little ways. Just over the hill—not more'n a mile and a half.

Miss Landen—A mile and a half, through this mud and splash! Well, if I don't need the grace of patience, I don't know who does. That man wrote nothing but truth, when he said, "Job mite have been the pashuntest man that ever lived—on *biles*—but he never taut skule and borded round."

[Miss Landen *puts on her bonnet and shawl, locks the school-room, and follows* Ike.]

[*Curtain.*]

Scene II.—Room in a "back woods" country farm-house. A table spread with supper—a dish of meat, potatoes, hot cakes; around which are seated, Mr. and Mrs. Jenks, Sally (in a flaming yellow "*polly-nay,*" and red calico skirt), Jake and Ike, and Miss Landen.

Mr. Jenks—Just fall to, and help yerself, school *mawm;* we don't have much manners here.

Sally—Now, par, *do* wait on the skule miss. Change the plates, *do.*

Mr. Jenks—Wal, ef I must, I'll hev to; but it's nuff site better for every one to look out for his own bread and dinner. (*Fills a plate with a piece of black-looking meat, a potato, and a huge buckwheat cake.*)

Mrs. Jenks—Dew yew take your tea with trimmin's, Miss *Lantern?*

Miss Landen—If you please. *Landen* is my name.

Mrs. Jenks—Oh, it is! Well, I didn't understand. Tom and Ike, do behave yerselves!

Tom—Give me a tater, then, I say I want a *tater.*
(*At the top of his voice.*)

Sally—Mar, Ike's a dippin' into my apple-sass. I wish you'd lick him, he acts awful.

Ike—I haint teched it! She's tellin' an awful whopper!

Mrs. Jenks—Go 'way from the table. I'll learn you to eat so, afore the skule mawm.

[*Seizes* Ike *by his collar, and drags him from the room, while he kicks and howls.*]

Mrs. Jenks—(*Returns, and seats herself again at the table*)—How on *airth* do you ever manage forty or fifty sich young-uns? I can't git along with two, and I'm allers powerful glad to git 'em off to skule in the mornin', and out of the way. Do try and make out yer supper, miss—goodness to gracious! I do believe Dan Jenks has given you the griddle greaser! (*Looking on* Miss Landen's *plate.*) He has, I swan! Now, Sally, that's too bad—some of your work, lettin' it drop in.

Sally—I jist laid it on the side of the meat-dish, and it slid in, I s'pose.

Mr. Jenks—I'm done; aint you, Jack? Come along and help me fodder the cattle.

[*Exit* Mr. Jenks *and* Jack—*all leave the table.*

Mrs. Jenks—Now, fly 'round, Sally, and help me do up the work, and then git the school *marm* to show you how to *croshay.*

[*Exit* Mrs. Jenks *and* Sally, *carrying dishes.*

Miss Landen—How shall I ever endure these horrid people until morning? How can I *ever* endure this mode of existence until the close of the term? I should like my vocation—the teacher's calling is a high and honorable one, even in a back-woods place like this—if I could have some place to call *home*. But this wretched system of boarding around. Ough! I wish the man who invented it had to live in this way for a ten years' term.

Enter SALLY. *Seats herself near* MISS LANDEN.

SALLY—Ef you'll show me that 'ere croshay stitch, I wish yew'd do it purty soon, for we "go to roost" airly here.

[MISS LANDEN *takes the needle and cotton, and endeavors to teach her, while the curtain falls.*]

[*Curtain.*]

ALICE'S PARTY.

CHARACTERS:—ALICE, large Girl.
GRACE,
KATIE, } little Girls.
TOTTIE,
WILL, an Interloper.

ALICE—Children, we are having a nice time this afternoon, and just for a change, suppose we all sit down and have a little talk, and each one tell what she would like best to have, either for a new plaything, for pleasure or comfort. Just think a little first. (*All musing.*)

GRACE—(*Very modestly speaks*)—I think if I had my wish,
I'd have a nice boy-dolly,
Dressed up in splendid soldier style;
I tell you, wouldn't he look jolly,

With suit of blue and buttons bright,
Upon his head a cap and feather,
A shiny gun—and on his back
A knapsack stuffed, and made of leather.

KATIE—*That would be nice.* Then *I* would like
A lady-doll, dressed to my fancy,
With top-knot, jockey feather, veil,
And "riding goat," like Cousin Nancy.
And then some day, when skies were bright,
And your gay soldier boy off duty,
They, too, could have a splendid drive,
To show off speed, and style and beauty.

ALICE—(*Interrupting gently*)—Now, girls, one thing
  you have forgot,
To carry out your plans, quite needful,
A something I have got to lend,
And you may use, if only heedful.
A nice new dolly-chaise for *two*,
And *you* must be the *pony* party;
I pray you take it when you choose,
And enjoy it with my wishes hearty.

GRACE and KATIE—(*In concert*)—We thank you dear,
  't is just like you
To be so thoughtful, loving too,
While we are heedless, gay and jolly,
While planning for each one's new dolly.

Enter WILL.

KATIE—Now here comes Will. I expect he's heard
All we have said—yes, every word.
Now tell us what you've got to say
About such trifles as girls' play.

WILL.—(*Putting on an air of great importance*)—Well—
I say:

  Away with all your dolly talk.
  Give me a little pile of money,
  And I will show you something smart
  And worth your care—*alive* and funny.
  I'd buy a pair of fine grey goats,
  I'd have them harnessed strong and **gaily**,
  I'd have a carriage, too, to match,
  And then, you see, I'd drive them daily.
  I'd take some *lady* by my side,
  But *not* a dressed up, *lifeless* dolly,
  But a real, gay, young chatterbox,
  Just like myself, so cute and jolly.
  Now what do you think?

  GIRLS—(*In concert*)—We think you're pretty **cute**, young sir,
And bound to make a noise and stir;
But when those splendid goats arrive,
Remember—we'll be ready for a drive.

  WILL.—(*Leaving the room*)—They had better wait till they are invited. Can't take so many.

  GIRLS—(*In concert*)—What a great man! A little selfish after all.

  ALICE—Well, here's little Tottie, she has said nothing only with her eyes. Now, darling, what would you like to have?

  TOTTIE—Me? I want—I guess I want
A pussy tat, a soldier, too,
A little box—a little doll.
I want most everything, *I do*.   (*Aside, softly.*)
But I want to ride with them goatees.

ALL—About the goatees, darling, we can't say, but all the rest you shall certainly have.

ALICE—A little more time yet, as the meeting folks say. Now for Katie.

KATIE—(*Hesitating*)—I have been thinking a good deal.
But like dear Tottie, 'mong so many,
I want most everything that's nice,
(I'd want them nice, or else not any).
I want a dress like Josie Fox,
I want a muff, a hat and feather,
I want some ribbons and some lace,
And a waterproof for rainy weather.
And then I want—I want—I want—
Oh, dear! I can't say what—I'm fearing
You think I am a foolish child,
And all my talk not worth the hearing.

ALICE—Never mind, we are not perfect yet.

GRACE—The clock says we must go pretty soon; but Alice, dear, has not told us a single wish yet.

ALICE—Never mind now, darlings. I have taken so much comfort in hearing you talk that all my selfish thoughts have fled away, so we will all be saying, "Good afternoon." (*Exchange of parting salutations.*)

[*Curtain.*]

WHO IS THE POET?

CHARACTERS:—MATILDA EVANS.
WILLIAM EVANS, her Brother.

SCENE.—MATILDA sits at a table writing.
Enter WILLIAM *with papers and letters.*

MATILDA—Oh, you're a good brother. Now I will see if my poem is published.

[*Opens a paper and looks it through.* WILLIAM *reads another paper.*]

MATILDA—No, it isn't here, and what is more, I don't believe they intend to publish it. Well, it is really like casting pearls before swine, to send anything good to these common editors. There is not one in twenty of them that knows a good poem when he sees it. If I were not so modest, and unassuming, I would send it to some of those periodicals whose editors do appreciate a good article. Ah! here are letters; I wonder who they are from. (*Opens one and reads. Throws it down angrily exclaiming:*) *Impudence!* I'll never send them a poem again so long as I live.

WILLIAM—What is the matter now, Matilda?

MATILDA—Matter enough, I should think. Just hear this letter from that impudent editor. (*Reads:*)

Miss Flora DeForest:

That's my *nom de plume*, you know.

Dear Miss:—

The enclosed poem which you modestly offer us for the trifling sum of ten dollars, we are obliged to decline. Your talent for writing poetry is, we admit, very uncommon, but as there are already so many poets in the literary field, we would advise you to try and see if your capacity is not equally good for washing dishes, and darning stockings. Yours with great regard,

E. T. TYPEMAN.

Matilda—Now, William, isn't that the most provokingly saucy letter you ever saw?

William—I don't see anything particularly saucy about it. He merely refused your poem, and gave you his professional advice.

Matilda—Professional advice, indeed! Nobody asked his advice. I'll show him that there's more than one editor in the world, and more papers than his little contemptible sheet. (*Seats herself at the table.*)

William—What do you propose to do, Matilda?

Matilda—I am going to send this poem to an editor who *does* know something. I think he will appreciate it.

William—Shall I tell you how to prevent the possibility of receiving from him a letter similar to this you have just received from Mr. Typeman?

Matilda—Yes, if you know. What shall I do?

William—Keep your poem at home, and follow the advice contained in this letter.

Matilda—That is about as much sympathy as I expected from you. I don't believe I am appreciated anywhere. (*Rises and walks.*) There, I have spent a whole week upon a poem which an insignificant editor refuses with scorn; and even here, at home, among my nearest and dearest friends, where I should meet with the sweetest sympathy, I am treated with coldness and indifference.

"Oh, for some heart to meet my own
In sympathy and love."

William—Stop quoting bad poetry. Let us talk plain prose. You say you are not appreciated here. Suppose you set the example, and commence by appreciating yourself. Your powers are not properly estimated, I'll admit, but you yourself have as false views of them as any one.

Matilda—I don't think I understand you.

William—Let me make it more plain then. You

have imagined you could write poetry, and sit here day after day, spending your time in scribbling sentimental songs which do not contain one word of sound common sense. The *jingle*, I'll admit, is well enough; the meter is not bad, but what does the whole of it amount to? Simply *highly embroidered nonsense*. This is why editors reject your poems. They have no heart in them. They don't mean anything.

MATILDA—Look at my verses about moonlight; I am sure they mean something.

WILLIAM—Yes, but let us hear a poem about daylight. Get up some morning and write a poem about sunrise, and perhaps it will be worth reading. Ah, Matilda, if you could only write such poems as Susie does, they would be appreciated by the folks at home, to say the least.

MATILDA—Susie? Why, William, what do you mean? I don't think she ever wrote two lines of poetry in her life.

WILLIAM—Nor did she, as *you* write poetry; and yet her daily life is one unceasing, and beautiful poem. No wandering, unwilling feet, or discordant syllables are in her poems, but a glad out-gushing of pure and loving inspiration is hers.

MATILDA—I know that Susie is a dear, good girl, but I never thought her poetical.

WILLIAM—That is because you do not understand what true poetry is. You fancy that you are a great admirer of Nature; but who ever saw you grafting roses, or training a vine? When were you able to name our common forest trees by looking at their leaves; or distinguish and name our garden birds by hearing them sing? Susie does this. Who plants and tends the flowers, making our little yard a perfect paradise of bloom and fragrance? Who knows where the sweetest wild blossoms are hid, and brings them to cheer the weary invalid? Who makes moss baskets for the windows, and picture frames for the parlor? Who binds up the broken limbs of lambs and chickens, and tenderly nurses them? Who reads for papa, sings for the baby, and resigns her own pleasure always for that of every other one? Who watches all of us when we are sick, with unceasing care? Whose feet are never weary while there is anything to be done for others? Whose hands are never idle so long as they can minister to the wants of a loved one? Is not Susie's unselfish life a beautiful poem, Matilda? And how much of such a poem are you living?

MATILDA—I can see it all, William, and it is very strange that I never thought of it before.

WILLIAM—You are not an isolated exception, Matilda. There are thousands of sweet, unselfish lives, whose sacrifices for others are accepted by them without even knowing or thinking that they *are sacrifices*, because made so freely and lovingly.

MATILDA—(*Putting away paper and pens*)—Brother William, you have opened my eyes to see myself in a true light, I believe, and I thank you for it. How idle and useless my life has been. I will scribble no more verses, but go to work and see if I can't do something *worth doing*. If I can not write poetry, I can at least help mother.

WILLIAM—That sounds like something sensible. When you have learned to do anything worth writing about, perhaps you will be able to write something worth reading. At any rate, you may depend upon one thing. The person who is not good for anything else, need not try to become a poet. That is my opinion. [*Exit.*

[*Curtain.*]

I GUESS I'M THE MAN.

CHARACTERS:—Mr. Hall, reformed Drinker.
Mr. Smith,
Mr. Jones,
Mr. James,
Mr. Rice, } Callers.

Scene.—Mr. Hall in his office alone, sitting at the table writing.

Mr. Hall—(*Taking up letter, reading aloud*)—"My dear sister, I hasten to inform you that I shall not annoy you any more by hard drink. I signed the pledge over six months ago, and have kept it to the very letter."

Enter Mr. Smith.

Mr. Smith—(*Interrupting reading, with a bow*)—Sir, can you inform me where Mr. Hall lives?

Mr. Hall—There are several families of Halls living around here. Which one do you wish to find?

Mr. Smith—I don't know his Christian name, but he is the father of two beautiful girls.

Mr. Hall—Really, sir, I can not tell which one you wish to find, as there are two families of Halls, and each has two daughters.

Mr. Smith—Just give me the addresses of both, as I am bound to get acquainted with them; but I don't think much of the old man.

Enter Mr. Jones.

Mr. Jones—Good evening. I call to see if you could inform me about a family by the name of Hall, and where he resides.

Mr. Hall—Are you acquainted with Mr. Hall?

Mr. Jones—No, only by hearsay.

Mr. Hall—Well, my friend, what have you heard?

Mr. Jones—I heard, and quite straight, too, that there

wasn't a harder drinker in town, and that he would die a genuine sot; but, then, he has two pretty girls.

Mr. Hall—Hem! hem! I guess that Mr. Hall has drank more or less; but, how about the girls?

Enter Mr. James.

Mr. James—Good evening, sir. I hope I'm not intruding.

Mr. Hall—Not at all, sir; what can I do for you this evening?

Mr. James—Do you know anything about a family by the name of Hall?

Mr. Hall—I'm slightly acquainted with two families by that name.

Mr. James—The Mr. Hall I wish to find, I hear has two girls just splendid, handsome and witty, but they don't take much after the old man.

Mr. Hall—What about the old man?

Mr. James—I hear he is drunk most of the time; and that he is a sharp, shrewd old man, and never was so drunk but that he could keep his money.

Enter Mr. Rice.

Mr. Rice—(*Addressing* Mr. Hall)—Good evening, sir. I beg pardon for intruding, but I'll detain you only a moment.

Mr. Hall—My friend, what can I do for you?

Mr. Rice—I just stepped in to see if you could inform me about a family by the name of Hall?

Mr. Hall—I think I can.

Mr. Rice—Please give me his address. (*Taking out his diary.*) I believe he has two daughters.

Mr. Hall—Yes; but they are quite shy.

Mr. Rice—I'll bet I can get acquainted; yes, and I'll bet I'll marry one of them.

Mr. Hall—You speak as though you should marry one, whether or no.

Mr. Rice—I tell you I am sure I shall, as the old man is rich. Yes, rich as a Jew; but he has been represented to me as being a close-fisted man, and not scrupulously honest in all his transactions in business, besides being drunk two-thirds of the time. Come, give me his address.

Mr. Hall—I do not think any of his friends here will be likely to get the old man's property—

[*Interrupted by all. Some exclaim*—What's that! What's that you say? *Others*—Why! why!]

Mr. Hall—For this very reason, I guess, I'm the man!

[*Curtain.*]

MISCHIEF.

DRAMATIC CHARADE.

CHARACTERS:—Grandpa.
Willie, } Grandchildren.
Kate,

Miss.

Scene I.—Willie *discovered whittling an arrow.*

Enter Kate, *with school-books, crying.*

Willie—Why! what's the matter with my sister Kate?
 I have not seen her cry of late.
Kate—(*Throwing down her books*)—These hateful books, there's not a leaf,
 But what's one constant source of grief;
 I try to learn my lessons every day,
 But the thoughts of sport have drawn my mind away:
 From all our childish plays I gain some bliss,
 But when my *lessons* come, I'm sure to *miss*.

WILLIE—Why, Kate, that's nothing—I've been at home
  all day,
   And what is more, I mean to keep away
   From books and school, till I can plainly see
   Some pleasure there in store for me;
   Then dry your tears; for eyes so red as this,
   Are not becoming to my little miss.
KATE—Don't call me *miss;* I hate the word,
   For which reproofs I've often heard;
   This very day, while in the Grammar class,
   My turn came round, I had to let it pass;
   "What!" growled the teacher, with a hideous frown,
   "You *miss* again, and can not parse a noun?"
   And then she thundered, with her usual sneers,
   "Unless you study more, you'll *miss* your ears."
WILLIE—Well, cheer up, Kate; no word I speak
   Shall start a tear across your cheek;
   But grandpa comes, and we must give report
   If we have spent our time in school or sport,
   Unless by some fair chance he fails to ask
   If we have learned or not our daily task.

Enter GRANDPA.

GRANDPA—How now, what do you there, my boy?
   What gives your fingers their employ?
WILLIE—I'm making, sir, an arrow for the bow
   That Uncle Joseph gave me long ago.
GRANDPA—And think you that, like William Tell,
   You'll shoot your arrow brave and well?
WILLIE—I do not know how well he shot.
KATE—Oh, tell his story, will you not?
   Do, Grandpa, tell us; take this chair,
   And I will place another there,

That you may rest your aching toe,
And tell his story. Don't say no.
  [GRANDPA *sits down:* WILLIE *and* KATE *come each side.*]
GRANDPA—Tell was a brave man over the sea,
Who wished to make all his countrymen free.
The usurper caught him, but spared him his breath,
On conditions almost as grievous as death.
Tell had a son, a small lad like you,
Who was, like his father, brave, loyal and true;
On the head of this boy a small apple was placed,
And two hundred yards the old tyrant paced
To measure the distance from father to son,
And show by what skill his life might be won;
And he told the brave man that his life he would give,
If he shot off the apple and let the boy live.
Then the archer took up his trusty cross-bow,
Selected an arrow as straight as a row,
Adjusted the string, and quickly it sped,
Well-aimed, at the apple upon the boy's head.
WILLIE—Did it miss?
KATE—Did it miss?
WILLIE *and* KATE—Oh! say, did it miss?
GRANDPA—What nonsense, my children, what nonsense is this?
Think you the fond father would ever aim
An arrow that might his only child maim?
No, Tell knew his skill, and the apple was found
In two parts divided; the boy was still sound.
Now, children, the lesson—remember this,
Be sure you are right, and never *miss.*
KATE—(*Aside to* WILLIE)—Does grandpa know what made me cry?

Grandpa—Now, youngsters, go and play, and I
  Will try to sleep, for should I miss my nap,
  My gouty toe might meet with some mishap.
Willie—Come on, then, Kate, and I will try my skill
  with this.   (*Holding up his arrow.*)
Kate—(*To audience*)—But no one would be hurt if he
  should *miss*.
  [Willie *and* Kate *go out.* Grandpa *leans back in
  his chair to sleep.*]

[*Curtain.*]

Chief.

Scene II.—Same as before. Grandpa feigning sleep.

Enter Willie.

Willie—(*Looks at* Grandpa, *runs to door, and calls:*)—
  Oh, Kate, come here; here's such a chance for fun;
  Don't mope along so slow, but run, Kate, run.
Kate—(*Outside*)—Why, what's the matter? why such
  haste?

Enter Kate.

Willie—Keep still, now, Kate, I've not a breath to waste:
  Grandpa's asleep, let's play him off a joke,
  As good as e'er his gouty slumbers woke.
Kate—What, Will, make fun of grandpa? Sure you jest,
  You can not, must not, thus disturb his rest.
Willie—He's slept enough. Now, do not silly be;
  Do as I bid, and leave the rest to me.
  I'll dress up like an Indian, tall and straight;
  And when he wakens up, I'll lie in wait,
  And frighten him till half his senses go,
  And gout forever leaves his aching toe.
Kate—Ha! ha! now, Willie, you're so dumpy small,
  You can not be an Indian straight and tall.

WILLIE—Well, well; then, Kate, I'll stand up in a chair,
    And say I'm *Chief*. 'T will give him such a scare,
    He'll tremble well from sole to crown,
    And think me a chief, and not a clown.
    Now, Kate, stand there and keep the flies away,
    Nor let one settle on a hair of gray;
    Let not his nose become a place of rest,
    He'd surely waken up and spoil my jest.
                                                 [*Goes out.*

KATE—Well, well I'll please him; but it's my belief,
    When grandpa wakes he'll whip the little *chief*.
        (*Walks on tiptoe, and brushes away the flies.*)

[*Enter* WILLIE *with feathers in his hat, bringing a red shawl or blanket, a hatchet, bow and arrow, and a pair of moccasins. Puts the moccasins down on the floor by a chair, gets up in the chair, and fixes the blanket round him so that it falls to the floor, and shows the moccasins sticking out. Holds the hatchet in his right hand, and bow and arrow in his left.*]

WILLIE—(*Hands* KATE *a string*)—Now, Katy, draw this string across his nose,
    He'll think it is a poison-spider's toes,
    And wake affrighted. Then I'll play my part,
    And he shall fear the *chief*, or feel his dart.

KATE—You will not hurt him, Willie, dear?

WILLIE—No, no; keep silent—never fear;
    And when he wakes with such a fright,
    My Kate must needs keep out of sight.
        [KATE *draws the string across* GRANDPA'S *face; he wakes, pretending to be frightened;* WILLIE *whoops, and* KATE *dodges behind* GRANDPA'S *chair.*]

WILLIE—(*In a gruff voice*)—When evil thoughts disturb the mind,
    The old man leaves his sleep behind,

And wakes to find his room possessed
By one who makes no mild request.
Old man, I am of many braves
The chief, the pale face idly craves
Our pity. Stationed all around
Are scores of men, who, at a sound
From me, would quick the old man take,
And burn him at the nearest stake.
But give me now a bag of gold,
And I will from your quiet fold
My braves withdraw, nor need you fear
That they shall e'er again come near.

GRANDPA—The old man totters near the grave,
And has no gold to give the brave.

WILLIE—My kin have gone beyond the flood,
The pale face steel hath drunk their blood;
Give me thy children, they'll atone,
For many wrongs the whites have done.

GRANDPA—Nay, take my life, but kindly spare
My children's children; they'd no share
In all thy wrongs; grant this relief,
And I will bless thee, haughty chief.

WILLIE—Your life, old man, is nothing worth,
Too long hath been thy stay on earth;
But, quickly bring to me the youth,
And I will give my word of truth
That they shall live. Else I will burn
Thy mansion, give my dogs a turn
At those fair children, and let thee live
To endure the pangs that I can give.

GRANDPA—Since naught can touch thy heart of stone,
I yield by brutal force o'ercome;
I go to bring them—God forgive,
If I have erred to let them live.   [*Exit.*

Kate—Oh, Will, how dared you scare him so?
　　He trembles—he can hardly go.
Willie—(*Getting down, and taking off his shawl*)—
　　I thought he'd sooner find me out,
　　What could the man have been about?
　　He'll soon come back, what shall I say?
　　I wish the *chief* could run away.
Kate—Nay, nay, brave chief; I bid you stand,
　　A *coward* chief would flee the land;
　　You've played the chief to scare your friends,
　　I'll be the chief to make amends.

[*Curtain.*]

Mischief.

Scene III.—Kate and Willie, as before.

Enter Grandpa.

Grandpa—(*Severely*)—Is this the chieftain bold and brave,
　　Who kindly vouched my life to save,
　　If I would give my children dear
　　To live in wigwams, slay the deer,
　　Their faces paint, their ears bedeck
　　With gewgaws, hung around their neck,
　　Or at their belt, the scalps they take
　　From slumbering foemen ere they wake?
Kate—(*Advancing half-way, and kneeling*)—Grandpa, forgive the naughty jest
　　With which we broke your sweetest rest;
　　The chieftain then so bold and brave,
　　Is willing now to be your slave,
　　So pardon us and take for fun,
　　What was in purest *mischief* done.

GRANDPA—Well, well, fair pleader, since you own
    Your foolish pranks, I'll not disown
    My children; but will take your hands
    In mine, and give you my commands.
                    (*Takes them by the hands.*)
    My children, you must never let
    Your love of *mischief* so forget
    What's due to age, that you would willing be
    To hang your grandpa to the nearest tree;
    But if you should, you'd better take a peep,
    And be quite sure that he is sound asleep.
WILLIE—Ah, grandpa, but I thought you smiled
    When giving up your children wild.
KATE—And I was sure you really knew
    Our Will's wild prank, and helped him through.
GRANDPA—(*To audience*)—Our charade's ended, but I'd like to add,
    That mischievous children are not always bad.
    Their faults lie on the surface; at the core
    Are many virtues, needing oft no more
    Than some kind hand to lead them on the road,—
    To show them what is evil, what is good;
    To quietly chide when pleasure lures too long,
    To make them love the right and shun the wrong.
KATE—And yet you'd best, like grandpa, when you sleep,
    For fear of *mischief* one eye open keep.

        [*Curtain.*]

UNCLE DEAL'S LECTURE.

CHARACTERS:—UNCLE DEAL, a crotchety old Bachelor.
MRS. DEAL, his Brother's Wife.
SCROGGINS, Mrs. Deal's Brother.
EDDIE, Mrs. Deal's little Son.
MISS DREWERY, a Caller.

SCENE.—UNCLE DEAL and his sister-in-law alone in the latter's parlor. A knock.

Enter SCROGGINS, *who, in attempting to bow, falls over a chair; a bottle rolls from his pocket, which he scrambles after and replaces.*

MRS. DEAL.—(*With an annoyed laugh*)—He's drunk! I say, it's too much to stand.

UNCLE DEAL—(*Approaching him*)—Allow me to escort you to the kitchen; you are at present hardly fit for parlor furniture.

[SCROGGINS *is led off the stage, looking very foolish, and making comic bows to the audience.*]

Re-enter UNCLE DEAL.

MRS. DEAL—(*In a rather loud and excited tone*)—Now, isn't that ridiculous. Scroggins might be ashamed of himself. There is not a finer man in these parts, if I am his sister, than Billy Scroggins when he's at himself, nor a worse one when the liquor's in and the wit's out.

UNCLE DEAL—H-m. That is usually the case, but I thought your brother had reformed, and all that sort of thing.

MRS. DEAL—So he had. He hadn't drunk a drop for three years, until Swiggins started that abominable tavern, right on his road from the shop. There was no manner of call for a public-house there; that is admitted by all. This thing of intemperance, it is awful, I say.

Uncle Deal—Its ravages are certainly fearful. It is not on the decrease, though, when a late calculation shows, in one of our most enlightened, refined and patriotic cities, nearly as many groggeries as lamp-posts.

Mrs. Deal—Well, the men seem to have grown perfectly indifferent on the subject, and what can women do. I will head a raid of women against it any time. I've read of such things being done, women breaking into whiskey shops, rolling the barrels into the street, staving in the heads, and letting the whiskey run down the gutter.

Uncle Deal—That way of proceeding doesn't seem to strike me as being very lady-like. But— (*A knock.*)

Enter Miss Drewery.

Mrs. Deal—How do you do, my dear Nellie? This is my husband's brother. (*Turning to* Uncle Deal, *and they exchange greetings.*) Do sit down, Nellie, and take off your things. I am sure you have come to spend the day with me.

Miss Drewery—Nothing would give me more pleasure if I had the time, but you know we are preparing a little surprise for brother Will when he comes home, in the shape of a little "sociable" at sister Annie's, and I just called to get the recipe for your currant wine. We all think it delicious.

Mrs. Deal—Well, sit down and talk to Uncle Deal, while I hunt up the recipe. If there is one thing I do brag on a little, Nellie, it is my currant wine. Oh! here comes Eddie, he'll entertain you while I'm gone.

Enter Eddie, *a little fellow of about seven years.*

[*Exit* Mrs. Deal.

Miss Drewery—Come and kiss me, Eddie, wont you? —that's a dear little fellow.

EDDIE—No, I shan't, though.

(*Clambers on* UNCLE DEAL'S *knee.*)

UNCLE DEAL—Now, Eddie, that's very impolite of you. You should certainly kiss the ladies when they ask you.

EDDIE—Would you? (*They both laugh.*)

Re-enter MRS. DEAL, *bearing a tray full of wine-glasses, filled with wine, which she hands around.* MISS DREWERY *accepts,* UNCLE DEAL *refuses.*

MISS DREWERY—How excellent.

[*Sipping it.* EDDIE *slyly helping himself to wine from the glasses on the sideboard.*]

MRS. DEAL—(*Producing the recipe, and handing it to her friend*)—You will see, there is a pint of brandy added to every two gallons of the wine. Do have some more, Nellie.

MISS DREWERY—Oh, no, thank you; indeed, I must go. Good morning, Mrs. Deal. Good morning, sir.

[*Exit* MISS DREWERY *with a bow.*

[EDDIE *begins to sing and caper around the room in a most extraordinary manner, to the consternation of his mamma, and amusement of* UNCLE DEAL, *who both try in vain to pacify him.*]

MRS. DEAL—(*Perceiving the empty glasses on the sideboard*)—Goodness, my boy! Did you drink all that wine?

UNCLE DEAL—Yes, I believe he did. (*Taking* EDDIE *in his arms, who must now feign sickness.*) He'll be quiet enough now for awhile, I think. (*Lays him on a sofa.*)

MRS. DEAL—(*Alarmed*)—Oh, how pale he is! I am afraid he will die. Do run for the doctor.

UNCLE DEAL—I don't think it's so bad as that. The stimulating effect of the liquor is dying away, and a violent reaction is taking place in the child's system. Presently he will fall into a heavy sleep; I think it is already creeping over him. There, I was right; he is going to sleep.

[MRS. DEAL *draws a deep breath, and resumes her sewing.* UNCLE DEAL *relapses into a meditative silence.*]

MRS. DEAL—(*After a pause*)—What in the world are you thinking of, Uncle Deal, you look so solemn?

UNCLE DEAL.—I am studying out the skeleton of a "Temperance Lecture," taking imaginary notes of the same.

MRS. DEAL—Oh, that would be excellent. I wish you would deliver it here in this town, and Swiggins would be one of the audience.

UNCLE DEAL—I have before me just the audience to whom I wish to address myself; though, would it were more numerous, if it were of the same character. In the unmeasured terms in which you have denounced poor Swiggins, justice compels me to denounce the domestic users of alcoholic stimulants. I condemn them *in toto.*

MRS. DEAL—(*With some warmth*)—Why, Uncle Deal, there isn't much alcohol in a little plain wine. Come, now.

UNCLE DEAL—Enough to make it intoxicating, as we have just witnessed. I insist upon it, if there were no refined drunkards, there would not be so many unrefined ones. "Total Abstinence" is the only true temperance motto. If I possessed the power, I would not only banish it from every public-house, but I would first dispense with its use in every private house. Come, Mrs. Deal, you were a very strong temperance woman this morning.

MRS. DEAL—What, then, would we do for brandy in our mince-pies, and wine in our sauces?

UNCLE DEAL—It strikes me that highly seasoned meat mixed with alcoholic drugs, and baked in greasy crusts, must be a most trying thing on the digestive organs, especially those of children, thus laying the foundation for a diseased and depraved appetite, which is the primary cause of so much drunkenness. If mince-pies were laid under ban, I believe it would be a blessing to the rising generation. It is astonishing that, while quackery and humbuggery of every sort count their dupes by thousands, the simple laws of physical health are so doubtingly and scoffingly received by the great mass of enlightened Christians. While our youth are instructed in all the lore of the ancient classics, they are suffered to remain in the grossest ignorance of that most wonderful organism, the human frame.

[*Curtain.*]

THE FAIRY QUEEN'S DECISION.

CHARACTERS:—HUBERT, a rich Boy.
PAUL, a poor Boy.
NANNIE, Paul's Sister.
FAIRY QUEEN.

SCENE.—A sitting-room. HUBERT discovered.

HUBERT—(*Soliloquizing*)—I hope that young scamp I met in the woods this afternoon will bring me the nest of young robins from the old apple-tree! Let me see, I promised him two dollars, these four silver fifty-cent pieces, for them—there will be three for himself, and one to dry the tears of little Nannie, who has threatened to cry her blue eyes out if any harm comes to them. One would think a bare-footed girl had rather have money than birds, and, as for Paul, what a nice Sunday hat he can buy!

Fairy Queen, make these bad, bad boys do better, and please put it into the hearts of these robins to love me just a little if I am ragged and barefooted!

FAIRY QUEEN—Yes, I swear by my scepter and by my star,
    They will love you, oh, darling child that you are!
    Paul, throw down your money, hie to your home,
    Or you'll change to an owl, through darkness to roam!
    Hubert, give to sweet Nannie the birds in your hat,
    Or to-morrow you'll wake, not a boy, but a bat.

HUBERT—(*Hands the birds over to* NANNIE, *and says, aside, to* PAUL)—Oh, my, what airs her majesty puts on!

NANNIE—(*Bending over the nest*)—O Fairy Queen, you are so good! What can I do for you?

FAIRY QUEEN—Love me, Nannie, only love me,
    And the angels bright above me,
    That are better still than I,
    Smiling downward from the sky,
    Will guard you, and, at death, will come
    To take you to their own bright home.

[*Curtain.*]

THE SECOND PRIZE.

CHARACTERS:—GRAHAM ALLCORN, a Tailor.
    JENNY ALLCORN, his Wife.

SCENE I.—A tailor shop. GRAHAM ALLCORN seated tailor-wise on a table, sewing.

GRAHAM—"Stitch, stitch, stitch, in poverty, hunger, and dirt." That's the way it is at this particular moment, and in this particular place. I stitch all day long and part of the night, and I think Thomas Hood must have had my humble self before his mind's eye when he penned that exquisite poem, "The Song of the Shirt." Now when a fellow works as hard as I do, it stands to reason that he ought to make a decent living—in fact he ought to live in pretty good style; but we don't live in good style. My wife has only common clothes, and my children's toes are beginning to peep out of their shoes. Well, there's one thing I'm sure of—if we aren't rich, we are comfortable. If we haven't plenty of money, we have contentment, and the Bible says, contentment is far better than wealth. I guess the Bible is right. Jenny and I are as happy a couple as can be found anywhere in the State, and the children seem to be happy too. Poor Benny is in the dumps, because he lost his place in the class yesterday, but that's nothing; he'll get over that. It will make him study harder, and if so, he will get up again. This coat is nearly finished. A few stitches more and I'm off for to-night. (*Hums a tune a few minutes.*)

Now there's that ticket in the Excelsior Gift Enterprise. If I should only draw the first, or the second, or the third, or the fourth, or even the fifth prize, would n't I be a rich man? Jenny laughs at the idea of my drawing anything. She says all Gift Enterprises are humbugs, but I think she's wrong. Jenny is generally right though; but I'm inclined to believe that she's wrong this time. I think the "Excelsior" is all right. Its promises are fair, and I think it is able to perform all it promises.

Enter JENNY, *her dress tucked up as if she had been working.*

GRAHAM—Halloo, Jenny, coming to see how I am getting along, are you? Nearly bed-time, isn't it?

JENNY—Yes, it's nine o'clock, and you must be tired. You've been working since daylight this morning.

GRAHAM—Yes, Jenny, I *am* sort of tired, but you know we must work or starve.

JENNY—Oh, I guess there's no danger of starving. We have enough to eat and enough to wear, and that is as much as we need. There's no use in having piles of gold; it only makes one feel unhappy.

GRAHAM—Yes, Jenny, that's what I was just thinking about. I was thinking that the Bible told us riches didn't make people happy, and that contentment was rather to be chosen than great riches, and the Bible is right, isn't it Jenny?

JENNY—Yes, Graham, it says, " Be content with such things as you have," and we ought to be. If we have gold we ought to be content, and if we have no gold we ought to be content. Now, there are the Joneses up the road; you know they've got a grand house and a grand farm, but the people say they do not get along well. They are quarreling continually, and the boys spend the most of their time in drinking and gambling. But, Graham, I had almost forgotten. Here's a letter for you. Benny got it as he came from school, but I forgot to give it to you at supper time. Open it and see what it is about. (*Hands letter.*)

GRAHAM—(*Taking it*)—A letter for me. I wonder who it can be from. As true as I live it is post-marked *New York.* It must be from Higgleson & Co., the proprietors of the Excelsior Gift Enterprise. (*Opens and glances over it.*) Hurrah, hurrah, hurrah! (*Jumps from table and dances around the room.*) It *is* from Higgleson & Co., and I have drawn the second prize. Hurrah, hurrah! Why don't you throw up your hat, Jenny? Why don't you shout? Why don't you dance? We are rich folks now. We are as rich as the Joneses, or the Harrisons, or the McNarys. Jenny, why don't you throw up your hat?

JENNY—Why, Graham, you are acting kind of shallow

like. I think you shouldn't make so much noise until you are sure of the prize. By the way, what is the second prize?

GRAHAM—It is a farm of two hundred acres in Virginia—that rich and fertile State—that home of the Presidents—that garden spot of the world! O Jenny, we are wealthy folks now! We needn't stitch and sew any more—we can live without working—we'll lead jolly lives—we'll go to the city, and live in a green stone front and ride in our carriage, and be as big as the biggest! Hurrah for Higgleson & Co., and the Excelsior Gift Enterprise!

JENNY—Graham, I believe you are a fool; we'll not go to the city. I'll *never* live in the city. I very much doubt whether your prize is of any account, but, if it is, we'll not sell it and go to the city; that I'm *sure* of. Do you think I'm a fool? I reckon I know what I'm doing. I'll live in the village; I'll have a nice little house on Main street; but as for going to the city, I'll *never* go, so that's settled.

GRAHAM—Well, Jenny, I guess we'll see about that. I guess *I'm* boss here. Who bought the ticket? I'd like to know, and who owns the farm? I'd like to know. I guess I can do as I please with my own property. I'll show you if I can't.

JENNY—And I'll show *you*. I am not going to allow you to go to the city, for if you do, you'd take to drinking and gambling just like the Jones boys, and you'd soon be on the broad road that leads to destruction. You're on that road *now*, Graham, and it is hard to tell what will become of you.

GRAHAM—Hold your tongue, I say, and leave the room.

JENNY—Yes, that's the way it is. (*Crying.*) Oh, has

it come to this? I am told to hold my tongue and leave the room. Well, I'll go right home to my father's, and then you'll see how fast you'll go down hill.

[*Exit crying.*

GRAHAM—What a dunce that woman is. She must kick up a fuss just about nothing at all. But she wont go to her father's, I know. I wouldn't care if she did. But I'll be off to bed now, and off to New York early in the morning. [*Exit.*

[*Curtain.*]

SCENE II.—A room in GRAHAM ALLCORN'S house.

Enter GRAHAM ALLCORN, *carpet-bag in hand.*

GRAHAM—Home again, and a pretty wild-goose chase I've had of it. Wont Jenny crow when she hears it all? By the way, I wonder where she is. She certainly wouldn't put that foolish threat of hers into execution, and go to her father's. It would make the old gentleman rage like a thunder-storm on a summer's evening. I suppose the children are at school. Well, I've been to school too, and learned a hard lesson, and a lesson I'll not soon forget. But here she comes!

Enter JENNY.

GRAHAM—Jenny, how do you do? Aren't you glad to see me?

JENNY—No; why should I be, when you told me to shut my mouth and leave the house?

GRAHAM—Ah, Jenny, so I did, but I was angry. Can't you forgive me? And if you will, I'll forgive you for talking so fiery to me. You know you rained it down pretty strong.

JENNY—Why don't you tell me about the second

prize? Did you sell the farm and buy a brown stone front, and a carriage, and a new suit? Tell me all about it.

GRAHAM—Ah, Jenny, I'm a sold man. The farm isn't worth a dollar.

JENNY—Why, how does that come? Didn't you say it was valued at fifty thousand dollars? I suppose you didn't let Higgleson & Co. cheat you out of it?

GRAHAM—Cheat! no! I'd like to twist their necks for them. The farm is made up of rocks and mountains, and isn't worth a copper. Hold on, Jenny, and I'll tell you all about it. I went to New York, as you know; and as soon as I got there, I rushed to the "Excelsior" office, and made some inquiries about the second prize. I tried to sell the farm to Higgleson & Co., at their valuation of it, and they laughed in my face. I then came down in my price, again and again, and finally offered it to them for five dollars. They said they didn't want it, and wouldn't have it. I gave them a piece of my mind, and then I came home; and here I am, less ten dollars in my pocket.

JENNY—And so your visions of a city life, and a brown stone front, have vanished.

GRAHAM—Truly they have, Jenny. Now, don't be old-womanish, and say, "I knew it would be so," but forgive me, and let us go on in the old way.

JENNY—I am willing, Graham, and I rejoice that it has turned out as it has. While we owned the two hundred acres, worth fifty thousand dollars, we were unhappy. We quarreled just like the rich Joneses up the road. Now we are poor again, and we'll be as happy as the days are long.

GRAHAM—Yes, Jenny, and we'll never forget the lesson of the "*Second Prize!*" [*Exit.*

[*Curtain.*]

WASHINGTON'S VISION.

A TABLEAU.

CHARACTERS:— { Thirteen Young Ladies, representing the thirteen Colonies.
Faith.
Hope.
Goddess of Liberty.
Washington.

Costumes.—The young ladies, representing the thirteen Colonies, should be dressed in black, badges of mourning; a silver band encircling the head of each, upon which is printed the name of the Colony which she represents.

Faith and Hope, white dresses, spangled with silver or gold colored stars. Paper of the same color, cut to imitate wings, pinned upon the shoulders. Bands upon the heads, with Faith printed upon one, and Hope upon the other.

Goddess of Liberty, with a blue trailing dress, white overskirt, and a red sash; a scalloped band upon the head, upon which is printed, Liberty. A United States flag in her hand.

Washington, dressed in black coat and pants, and white vest; pants short, buckled just below the knee, with a steel or silver buckle; long, white stockings, low shoes and steel buckles.

—A sleeping apartment. Washington upon a couch, asleep. Colonies, at a short distance from the couch, standing in a semicircle, forms slightly bowed, looking down upon the floor. A chain, extended in front of them, as if fastened upon the wrists of the Colonies, but so arranged that it can be dropped instantly.

[*Let some one behind the Curtain read these words:*]

"I am weary with my groaning. All the night I water my couch with my tears. Mine eye is consumed because of grief. The enemy persecutes my soul; yea, he treads down my life upon the earth; he lays mine honor in the dust. I am troubled, I am bowed down greatly. I go mourning all the day long. I have roared by reason of the disquietness of my heart."

[*Enter* Hope *and* Faith, *walking to the head of* Washington.]

Hope—(*Bending down, apparently whispering in his ear, while these words are read:*)—"Why art thou cast down, O Washington? Why is thy soul disquieted within thee? Hope thou in God, for thou shalt yet praise Him for the help of His countenance."

FAITH—(*Pointing upwards, while the reader continues:*) —"I cried unto the Lord with my voice, and He has heard me out of His holy hill. I will not be afraid of ten thousand of people that have set themselves against me round about. Thou wilt save the afflicted people. Thou wilt bring down high looks. Blessed be the Lord God, who doeth wondrous things. By Him I can run through a troop, and by my God can I leap over a wall. He teacheth my hands to war, and my fingers to fight. I have pursued my enemies, and overtaken them. I shall not turn back until they are consumed. They have fallen under my feet, and are not able to rise. The chains of oppression are broken, and I am delivered from their power."

[*Chains fall from Colonies.* FAITH *and* HOPE *vanish quickly.*]

Enter GODDESS OF LIBERTY.

[GODDESS OF LIBERTY, *waving banner, takes her stand at the head of* WASHINGTON. *Colonies surround the couch.* GODDESS OF LIBERTY *waves banner over all, while they sing the* "Star Spangled Banner." *Instrumental music, if desired.*]

[*Curtain.*]

CURING AN INVALID.

CHARACTERS:—AUNT JANE, an Invalid.
JULIA,
IDA,   } her Nieces.
AMANDA,
MRS. GREEN, Neighbor.

SCENE.—A neatly furnished room; an old lady in an easy chair.

AUNT JANE—Well, here I am left all alone, and just as sick as I can be, and them good-for-nothing girls gadding about somewhere, and I'll declare, it's 'most eight o'clock, and I've no breakfast yet. Well, well, well, that's what I call gratitude, after all I've done for them. I'll not put up with it; so there. (*She rings violently, and calls* MANDY, IDEE, *and* JULEY.) Can't some of you come?

Enter three girls. JULIA, *with a wash bowl of water and a white towel, kneels down for* AUNT JANE *to wash.* AMANDA *with a fan.* IDA, *with a comb and brush, combs* AUNT JANE'S *hair.*

AMANDA—(*Fanning her aunt*)—Why, aunt, are you well enough to be up so early this morning?

AUNT JANE—Up so early! I should think it wasn't so early, when I've been up three mortal hours!

IDA—Oh, aunt, three hours!

AUNT JANE—(*Snappishly*)—Yes, three hours. What is there strange about that?

JULIA—It isn't eight yet, aunt, and you told us to call you at eight.

AUNT JANE—Well, what if I did? You might have looked in to see if I wanted anything.

IDA—I did come in at six, and at quarter after seven, and you were sound asleep—

AMANDA—And snoring away like everything. O aunt, what a funny snore you've got!

AUNT JANE—Snoring, snoring! Oh, you wicked little wretch. I never did snore in my life. Never, never.

ALL THE GIRLS—(*Laughing*)—We thought you did.

AUNT JANE—Thought I did! Well, perhaps you think I don't want anything to eat to-day.

JULIA—Oh, yes, aunt, I have your breakfast almost ready.

AUNT JANE—And pray what have you got to make such a fuss about?

JULIA—Tea, toast, fresh eggs,—

AUNT JANE—There now, I knew it. I never can have anything I want.

IDA—What do you want, aunt?

AUNT JANE—I want some gruel, and you all know that.

JULIA—Yes, aunt, and I have gruel, too.

AUNT JANE—Well, for mercy's sakes, why didn't you say so? Go and bring it; don't stand there all day.

(JULIA *goes out, but soon returns with a bowl.*)

JULIA—Here is your gruel, aunt, and I do wish you would try to eat the toast and eggs.

AUNT JANE—(*Taking the bowl, tasting daintily*)—Here, take it away; it's as salty as brine. Mercy, mercy me! Oh, dear!

[JULIA *goes out, but soon returns with a nice, tempting breakfast on a large waiter, covered with a white cloth.*]

JULIA—Here, aunt, is your breakfast, and some fresh gruel I hope you can eat.

AUNT JANE—(*Tasting again*)—O Juley, it haint a single bit of salt in it now. Was there ever such a poor, neglected creature as I am!

Ida—Dear aunt, do try to eat something. Julia spent nearly all the morning trying to cook you something nice.

Amanda—Yes, and I took some of old Skinflint's apples for you.

Aunt Jane—You did, hey? And pray, who gave you permission to take other people's apples?

Julia—I asked Mr. Green for them.

Amanda—And he told us to take as many as we wanted, and when I went to get them, old Skinflint (his wife, you know) squalled out at me to let her apples alone. O aunt, if you was such an old, mean, stingy thing as she is, I'd, I'd—

Aunt Jane—Well, miss, what would you do?

Amanda—I'd get married, that I would. Why, aunt, she ordered me home, and said I was stealing her apples, and she would call and tell you on me to-day.

Aunt Jane—She did, hey? Well, let her come, we will see. Let her tell me you stole! (Aunt Jane *eats heartily, drinks her gruel, and keeps repeating to herself:*) My girls steal! We'll see.)   (*Some one knocks.*)

Aunt Jane—Here, girls, take this away. Idee, give me my walking stick. We'll see. My girls steal, indeed!   [*Exit* Julia, Ida *and* Amanda.

Enter Mrs. Green, *a tall, lean, lanky, shabby-looking woman, with a pipe in her mouth.*

Aunt Jane—Good morning, Mrs. Green.

Mrs. Green—Good morning. I haint no time to stop. I jist stepped over to tell you that your girls has been in my orchard a—

Aunt Jane—Just stop a moment, Mrs. Green. You might say something that would hurt my feelin's; I'm tender, been sick, you know; besides, I want to know who stayed with you and sat up of nights to let you sleep, when you was broke down, a-waiting on your sick old man last summer?

Mrs. Green—You did, ma'am, but—

Aunt Jane—Hold on; who stayed with you? who carried you butter, fresh eggs, and so on, when you had none?

Mrs. Green—Your girls.

Aunt Jane—Who helped you drive the cattle out of your orchard? Who lifted heavy rails to fix the fence, when your old man was down?

Mrs. Green—Your girls; but it don't become you to be a tellin'—

Aunt Jane—Well, now, I want you to shet up and go home, and remember, if I scold my girls, I don't 'low nobody else to scold them.

Mrs. Green—I will have my say, 'low or no 'low. If they did do all that, I haint gwine to have them a stealin' my apples—

Aunt Jane—(*Jumping up, drives* Mrs. Green *out of the room, whipping her over the shoulders with her walking stick*)—Steal! my girls steal, hey? Steal indeed!

(*The three girls come from behind a screen laughing.*)

Amanda—Our aunt dined, drank grew-well (*gruel*), and whipped Mrs. Green! Hurrah for Aunt Jane!

[*Curtain.*]

LITTLE FOLK'S OPINIONS.

CHARACTERS:—ANNIE LEE, } Two little Girls.
BIRDIE BELL,

SCENE.—ANNIE and BIRDIE, sitting very close together.

ANNIE—Didn't you know, Birdie, I'se dot a new dollie? My dranmuzzer div it to me on Tris'mas day.

BIRDIE—And I'se dot a new dollie, too, and a pair of new shoes, and a 'ittle box and a tup and a saucer, and ever so many ozzer tings. Oh, my, but I does have the fun a-p'ayin' wiz zem.

ANNIE—Tum down to our house some day, and I'll show you my new dollie and a whole heap of ozzer tings. My dollie's dot sich pitty eyes and sich rosy cheets, and oh, sich a funny nose. It dist mates me feel dood all over to loot at it.

BIRDIE—It was my Untle Don yat dive me my new dollie. I tell 'oo my Untle Don is a real nice old man, I like him, oh, ever so much. Last Fantsdiven' he buyed a bid turkey and div it to ma, and she would a tooked it for a Fantsdiven' dinner, but her and pa, and Untle Don and me was inyited to do to a Fantsdiven' up at Untle Yeuben's, and so we didn't have our turkey, for Untle Yeuben's folts said we must besoor and do, and ma said Aunt Yachel and Untle Yeuben would both be hoppin' if we didn't do. I didn't know yat Aunt Yachel and Untle Yeuben tould hop. I dis tought it was 'ittle folts like you and me yat hops, and when I yent down on Fantsdiven' I ast Aunt Yachel and Untle Yeuben if dey had been a hoppin' any lately. Untle Don he jist laughed and laughed, and Aunt Yachel said dey used to pay at hop, step and jump when dey was 'ittle, but dey hadn't p'ayed any at it yately. Then Untle Don he jist ho-hoed and haw-hawed awful, and Untle Yeuben said he didn't sink there was much to laugh about. I'd ast more about the hoppin', but muzzer toot me out of the room awful twick jist lite she tot I was sit or had the tolic or somethin'. When we was out she telled me not to say nussin' more about the hoppin', and I didn't say nussin' more 'bout it.

ANNIE—We had a turkey on Fantsdiven', too, and it was a dolly big feller. Our Harry he's dot to sayin' big words now, and he said it was a *rooter*. I don't know what a rooter is, but muzzer said for Harry to hush and not say sich words as yat. Harry said it wasn't a swear-word, but muzzer wouldn't a'yow him to say it anyhow, as it wasn't a nice word. Harry said he dot it from Frank Dones, and I des Frank's a nice enough boy. He smotes a cidar, and is dittin' to feel pitty big. Harry said Frank was talkin' about Mr. Smith, and he said he was a rooter. I don't lite 'ittle boys as smotes cidars, do you?

BIRDIE—No, I'm soor I don't. Cidars mates boys have sich a bad smell. I hate the smell of tobatto. My Untle Don smotes. I sink I'd lite him a dood 'eal better if he wouldn't smote.

ANNIE—I dess I'll have to do home now. Let us do and see if our muzzers are still talkin' to each ozzer. My! but dey do talk fast when dey dit togezzer.

BIRDIE—Annie, I lites you a heap, and I'se doin' to dive you sumsin.

ANNIE—You are! Oh, doodie! what is it?

BIRDIE—Tum on and I'll so it to you. I tink you'll be so dlad you'll dump up and down.   [*Exit.*

[*Curtain.*]

THE DOCTOR'S CHOICE.

CHARACTERS:—MARY LOWE, a poor Dress-maker.
MAGGIE, her invalid Sister.
MISS SMITH, Lady of fashion.
DR. DANE, Maggie's physician, and admirer of Miss Smith.

SCENE I.—A plain room in a dark, narrow street.

MAGGIE—I've been thinking, sister Mary, of our old home on the hill,
Where your face was round and rosy, and the nights were always still;
I'm so wearied, since this illness, of the loud talk in the street,
Of the roll of wagons past the house, and the constant tramp of feet.
I'm so tired, Mary, tired, that the fretful words will come; (*Anxiously.*)
Why wont you leave this noisy place—why wont you take me home?

MARY—Why, my dear child, how grieved I am to hear these words from you! (*Lays aside her work.*)
I'll lay aside my work awhile. What would you have me do?
You will not grieve me long, I'm sure, by these impatient ways;
You know the same God rules the storm that rules the pleasant days.
Have you forgotten Him whose love has been the orphan's stay,
And that it is the same wise love that's darkened all the way?

MAGGIE—No, Mary, no, I know 'tis so; but sinful thoughts will come,
When I lie helpless, watching you, and think of our old home.
You know there was no sickness there, you did not toil for bread;
And what was once all light and love, is want and pain instead.

MARY—But God has wrought this change, my child, we would not wish it so.
Should we question what He does? He can not err, you know.
No, darling, though this fearful night be deep, and dark, and long,
Though we be weary on the way, God's grace shall make us strong.
Now close those aching eyes awhile, for I must work to-night;
Trust all the future to our God, we know He'll make it right. (*Some one taps lightly and opens the door.*)

Enter MISS SMITH.

MISS SMITH—Good evening, Miss: I've called to see if all my work's complete;
I sadly fear I've soiled my skirts on this dark, narrow street (*Shakes her clothes.*)

MARY—(*Setting a chair*)—I'm grieved, Miss Smith, to say to you what I have said to none;
The work I promised you to-night now lies but partly done.

MISS SMITH—(*Angrily*)—Is that so, Miss? indeed, indeed!
I wonder what excuse you'll plead.

Mary—Miss Smith, my sister, being ill, has called for constant care;
I've given your dress all the time that this sick child could spare.

Miss Smith—Well, I can't be put off like this; since illness takes your time,
You best had tend the sick one's needs, nor strive to tend to mine. (*Sits down.*)
Please do my work up, nor expect, for work you've done before,
Remuneration, since the task of having this made o'er.
(*Shakes the half-finished dress.*)

Mary—(*With some excitement*)—Young lady, wait, please hear me through; not for myself I speak,
But for my suffering sister there, so pale, so frail and weak.
Day after day I've planned and toiled through this hard, trying spring,
To appease a poor, sick sister's wants by what this toil would bring.
And has it been in vain, Miss Smith, must this child suffer on,
Because my hands have failed to do all that you would have done? (*Weeps.*)

Miss Smith—(*Taking out her purse*)—Ah! quite a scene indeed, indeed! Here is a silver dime,
'Twill buy you bread for quite a while, and keep you for a time.

Mary—(*Looking up with indignation*)—I am not asking alms, Miss Smith, and each cent should be spurned,
From your full purse, unless it's what you justly think I've earned.

Door opens, and DR. DANE *enters.*

MISS SMITH—(*Rising and appearing to be confused*)—
You here, indeed! how shocked I am! I really can
not see—

DR. DANE—(*Smiling and shaking hands*)—And I am
equally surprised that this strange thing should be.
(*Turning suddenly to* MARY, *exclaims:*)
And what means this, my friend? These tears—is my
young patient worse?
(*Looks at* MAGGIE *and smiles.*)
You know the blues will never do for doctor or for nurse.
(*Goes to* MAGGIE, *who is also weeping.*)
What means this, ladies? Pray explain—why this great
grief to-day?
I think it's best that I should know; explain it, Nettie,
pray. (*Turning to* MISS SMITH.)

MISS SMITH—(*Curling her lip scornfully*)—I do not
feel in duty bound to explain pauper grief,
Nor give an inexperienced guess at what might bring
relief.

DR. DANE—(*Appearing grieved*)—Miss Smith—
Annette—I am shocked! This talk will never do.

MARY—Dr. Dane, 't is proper, sir, I should explain to
you.
I have been sewing several weeks for this young lady, sir,
I'd promised work complete to-night, and I've disappointed her.

MISS SMITH—(*Rising*)—Please have my work all
ready, Miss, my servant soon will call;
(*To* DR. DANE.)
I'll leave here now—then, Dr. Dane, you'll hear the
story all.

MARY—(*Quietly*)—You judge unjustly; truly, ma'am,
  I've nothing more to say;
Your work I'll see is well prepared when the servant
  calls. Good-day.
            (MISS SMITH *bows superbly and goes out.*)
              [*Curtain.*]

SCENE II.—MAGGIE sits up looking brighter.

Enter DR. DANE, *smiling.*

DR. DANE—Ah! better, Maggie—this I know by the
  bright light in your eyes—
Full well enough, your sister says, for a wonderful surprise.
You know your old home on the hill, you've loved so
  well and long,
I've bought that very place to-day—this news must make
  you strong;
Because—oh, here's the lady now, all blushes, too, you
  see,
Who's promised to be mistress there, (*taking her hand,*)
  and walk through life with me.

MAGGIE—(*With much confusion*)—Why, Mary—Dr.
  Dane—indeed! I thought Miss Smith—you
  know—

DR. DANE—Yes, my dear child, we understand, and
  rejoice that 'tis not so.
Maggie, that lady's real, true heart, in its benighted state,
Was, happily, unveiled to me before it was too late.
Her proud and selfish ways, my child, God meant they
  should be learned;
But the measure that she's meted out we would not
  wish returned.

MARY—No, while we are offering thanks to-day, for this great joy we find,
We'll pray that Heaven's pure, perfect rays may pierce her darkened mind.

[*Curtain.*]

THE UNWELCOME GUEST.

CHARACTERS:—EDWARD SIMPSON.
MRS. EMELINE SIMPSON, his Wife.
JOHN SIMPSON, his Brother, and a Guest.
MARTIN JONES.
MRS. ELIZA JONES, his Wife.

SCENE.—A room in EDWARD SIMPSON'S house. MR. and MRS. SIMPSON discovered.

MRS. SIMPSON—Edward, I may just as well say plainly that I think we must do something to get your brother off our hands. He has been here now over two weeks, and he stays and stays just as if this was his home, and as if he hadn't the slightest idea of ever going away.

EDWARD SIMPSON—You are quite right, wife; we must get him away. I thought it possible, when he came here, that he had plenty of money; but that idea has vanished entirely. If he had money, he would not go around so shabbily dressed. He had the audacity to hint to me, yesterday, that I might buy him a new coat; just as if I hadn't enough to do to buy new coats for myself and my children.

MRS. SIMPSON—Oh, the impudence of some people! I am sure we have done very well in keeping him these two weeks, and not charging him a cent for his boarding. And now he wants a new coat, does he? I wonder he didn't ask for a full suit; he certainly has need of it; but he needn't expect to get it here. But are you *sure*, Edward, that he didn't bring any money home with him?

EDWARD SIMPSON—Yes, quite sure. I didn't say any thing to him about it, but John was never the man to go in rags if he had any money in his pocket. He has been away for fifteen years, you know, and he might have made plenty of money in that time; but it is my impression, that if he did make any thing, he spent it all before he started for home.

MRS. SIMPSON—Well, what are we to do with him?

EDWARD SIMPSON—Send him to the poorhouse, I suppose. I don't quite like to do that, either; for people *will* talk, and they will say I ought to have kept him in his old days.

MRS. SIMPSON—Let them talk. It's nobody's business but our own, and it will all blow over in a week or two. Of course we can't have him on our hands as long as he lives, merely because the neighbors will talk a little about our sending him to the poorhouse.

EDWARD SIMPSON—No, of course not. Here he comes now; we must inform him of our decision.

Enter JOHN SIMPSON, *shabbily dressed.*

EDWARD SIMPSON—John, we have been talking about you.

JOHN—So I supposed. I thought I heard my name mentioned. You were considering that matter about the coat, were you? I hope you will think favorably of it.

MRS. SIMPSON—(*Bridling up*)—No, sir; we were not thinking of buying you a coat, but we were speaking of your audacity in making such a request.

JOHN—Ah! were you? Don't you see I am old now, and dreadfully crippled with rheumatism? And, of course, I am not able to work to buy myself clothes. If my brother will not take care of me now, who will?

Mrs. Simpson—That's just what we are going to talk about.

Edward Simpson—Wife, allow me to speak to John about this matter. (*To* John.) It may sound a little harsh and unpleasant, but we have come to the conclusion that we can not keep you any longer. You know we are not very well-off in this world's goods; we have not much house-room, and we have three children that demand our attention. We have kept you two weeks, and we think we have done very well. We feel that you would be considerably in our road here, and we have concluded to send you to the poorhouse.

John—The poorhouse! I always did hate the poorhouse. It must be so lonesome there; and then, I don't think the boarding will be good. Must I go to the poorhouse?

Edward Simpson—Yes, we have decided. We can not keep you.

John—I thought, when I was away, that if I could only get home again, I would find my brother willing to take me under his roof, and allow me to end my days there. But I was mistaken. When must I go?

Edward Simpson—I will have the papers made out, and be ready to take you to-morrow afternoon.

John—Send for Eliza Jones and her husband. They will not want to keep me, either, I suppose—how can I expect them, when they are a great deal poorer than you? But send for them. I want to see them, and say good-bye, before I go away.

Edward Simpson—Emeline, tell Parker to run across to Jones' for his Uncle Martin and Aunt Eliza.

[*Exit* Mrs. Simpson.

JOHN—If they do not treat me well at the poorhouse, what shall I do? Cut stick and run off, or sue them for breach of promise?

EDWARD SIMPSON—(*Aside*)—It seems to me, he takes it exceedingly cool. But it is better he should do so, than to make a noise about it. (*To* JOHN.) I think you will be well treated. The Superintendent is very kind to all under his care, and is considered a perfect gentleman.

JOHN—A gentleman! I'm glad of that. (*Sarcastically.*) Ah! Edward, it is a great thing to be a *gentleman*.

EDWARD SIMPSON—I am glad you are willing to go without making any fuss about it. You know people *will* talk; and they would talk a great deal more, if you should be opposed to going. I hope you will not think unkindly of us, because we have concluded to take this step; you see we can not well keep you here; and as you are getting old, and are greatly afflicted with rheumatism, you will be better attended to there than you could be here.

JOHN—Yes, yes, I understand. Don't fret about me, Edward. I suppose it isn't much difference where I live, and where I end my days. But, Edward, I *think* I would not have treated you so. However, one hardly knows what one will do when one comes to the pinch. If I had brought home a market-basket full of ninety-dollar gold-pieces, perhaps I would not have taken up so much room in your house, nor crowded your children so dreadfully.

Enter MRS. SIMPSON, *and* MR. *and* MRS. JONES.

MRS. JONES—(*Running to* JOHN)—O John, my brother, they want to send you to the poorhouse! You shall not go! you shall not go!

MARTIN JONES—No, John, you shall not go. While we have a crust of bread, you shall share it with us.

John—But I never did like to eat crusts.

Mrs. Simpson—That's him, for you! He doesn't want to pay anything for his board, but he wants to have the best.

John—And he doesn't like to eat dirt.

Mrs. Simpson—Do you mean to say that I am a dirty cook?

John—(*Whistles "Yankee Doodle"*)—Come, if I am to go to the poorhouse, let me be off.

Mrs. Jones—You shall not go. We are poor, but you shall stay with us. We can find room for you, and we will be provided for, I'll warrant, someway.

Mrs. Simpson—People oughtn't to be rash about taking on a load they can't carry.

Edward Simpson—Emeline, if Martin and Eliza want to keep John, let them do so; don't say a word. Of course, I think they have quite enough to do to keep their own heads above water; but if they want to keep John, it is their own business.

John—Yes, it is their own business; and if they were on the point of sinking, would *you* raise a finger to keep their heads above water? *No!* Edward—I can not call you brother—I know you now. I leave your house to-day, but I do not go to the poorhouse. I have money enough to buy and *keep* a hundred such little farms as yours, and a hundred such *little men*. I do not need your coats nor your cringing sympathies; I wanted to find you out. I wanted to know what kind of a man you were, and *I know*. When I came home, I determined to find out, in some way, whether you or the Jones family were most deserving of my money. I have found that out; and I go with them, to make my home there.

Mrs. Simpson—But we didn't know—

John—Ay, I know it. You thought I was a beggar;

you thought I had no money, and no clothes. If you had believed otherwise, you would have received me with open arms. Come, (*To* MR. *and* MRS. JONES,) we will go. I shall not forget you for your kindness. I will make my home with you; and if it is true, that you have had hard enough work to keep your heads above water, it shall be so no longer. (*To* MR. *and* MRS. SIMPSON.) I had almost forgotten. Here are twenty dollars, for my two weeks' board. (*Throws down the bills.*) You see that although I may have a *shabby appearance*, I am yet able to pay my way in the world. Good-day, Mr. and Mrs. Simpson.

[*Exit* JOHN SIMPSON, *and* MR. *and* MRS. JONES.

EDWARD SIMPSON—Confound the luck!
(*Rushes out at one side of the stage.*)

MRS. SIMPSON—Isn't this dreadful!
(*Rushes out at the other side of the stage.*)

[*Curtain.*]

NOT WHAT HE WANTED.

CHARACTERS:—JOE, an impatient Boy.
MYRA, his Sister.
MARTIN, } his Companions.
HENRY, }

SCENE —A sitting-room on a hot summer day.

JOE—(*Solus.*)—Oh, dear me! What shall I do? I really believe I shall melt. (*Fanning himself with his hat, and puffing furiously.*) I can't stand such awful heat, and I never saw such hot weather before. It is enough to melt the whole human race. I wonder what such weather was made for. Phew! I can't stand it any longer, (*pacing and blowing around the room,*) and there's no use of talking. Why, I shall melt; but how it would look if I should indeed melt and turn into a pot of grease! But see how I sweat; and see how red my face is. (*Wiping his face while he looks in a glass.*) Man was never made to endure such weather, for I am sure if I get much hotter I shall certainly be *hissing* hot. My handkerchief is as wet as a dish-cloth, and looks pretty much like one. The cologne has all vanished, and no wonder at it; all been dissipated into vapor by the heat of such a furnace; and, like it, I am going as fast as possible. I don't believe I weigh half as much as I did in the morning, for I can almost lift myself by my boot-straps, and, if I were not so hot, could throw myself by them over a stone wall. Oh, dear, what shall I do? I *can't* stand it any longer.

(*Making a great noise, stamping around the floor.*)

Enter MYRA.

MYRA—Joe, what in the world is the matter with you? What is all this fuss and noise about?

JOE—If you were only half as hot as I am, you would soon find out what it is all about. I believe the world is coming to an end; I know it is burning up!

MYRA—Oh, you great dunce to make such a hurrah about warm weather. Why don't you sit down and be quiet? You are in such a *stew* you will never become cool.

JOE—I guess if you were half as hot as I am, you would make a bigger fuss. Oh, how I wish I were in Greenland, Iceland, or astride the North Pole, or hugging an iceberg; only that I might get cooled off a little.

MYRA—What a great crazy lubber for a boy of fifteen, to make such an outrageous ado about a little summer weather!

Joe—Get away with such insults when I am suffering so severely; I wont endure it.

Myra—But what will you do about it? The heat is just as great in my case as in yours. What if I should go storming around as you do; and all the rest of our folks should do the same; what a bedlam we should have!

Joe—Now you leave the room if you have no more sympathy for a suffering brother than this. You are around here as cool as an ice-cream plate, and only wish to *insult me* as if I were your slave.

Myra—Insult you! I simply said that I am exposed to the heat of the weather as much as you are, which is true, and you call that insulting! But more than this, I have been in the kitchen over the fire helping to get your dinner, while you have only had to make yourself comfortable as best you could, and then you charge me with being cool as an *ice-cream* plate, in a most insulting way. Is this fair?

Joe—I don't care, you don't suffer as much as I do. The heat of the kitchen is nothing compared to this.

(*Sighing heavily.*)

Myra—Then you had better go into the kitchen yourself if that is any help. I only wish you would. If standing over the hot stove as I did wouldn't take some of the *blubber* out of you, then I will set myself down for a dunce.

Joe—Oh, you are the greatest torment in the world—

Myra—Greater than the heat you are suffering from?

Joe—You only wish to torment me while in this plight. What do I care if you have been over the hot stove? Perhaps the heat does not affect you so severely as it does me. You can strut around with *laces* and thin dresses, the coolest things in the world. No wonder the heat does not discommode you.

Myra—Why don't you put on such refrigerators then? You certainly can try them, and the experiment wouldn't hurt you, since you think them to be so excellent.

Joe—Oh, you are a contemptible pest! See my handkerchief! (*Holding it up.*) See how it is soaked!

Myra—Yes, it would do admirably to cover a kite for all the wet there is in it. But how it is stained!

Joe—Yes, the berry juice is stewing through with the perspiration. It's those berries we had for dinner.

Myra—You great goose, it's where you spilled your berries over it. Ha, ha! Berry juice coming through the pores of the skin! Who ever heard of such a ludicrous idea before?

Joe—There, everything I say must become the matter for one of your jests. I wish, if you can not come with a ray of comfort, you would stay away with your contemptible jokes.

Myra—You must not say such foolish things then. It is enough to make a marble statue laugh to hear such nonsensical remarks from a young man so *professedly* smart as Joe Prettyman. Why don't you sit down and be quiet; or busy yourself about something? then you would not think of hot weather. It will soon be evening, and the cool breezes will remove the intensity of the heat; then how very simple all this conduct of yours will appear.

Joe—I don't care, I can't stand it much longer. I am almost melted. I feel real faint.

(*Leaning against the wall.*)

Myra—Come and sit down here and I will fan you. But, see! there are Henry and Martin coming through the yard with some ice, I should think.

Joe—(*Quickly reviving*)—Oh, that's good! and if I don't have some of it, then my name isn't *Joe*.

Myra—Well, I wouldn't be so excited about it; and

don't go to being mean with them, or you may be sorry for it.

JOE—Yes, now you had better turn preacher! Don't you suppose I have a bit of common sense?

MYRA—(*Looking towards them*)—I should think they have some ice in a glass jar. How delightful on such a warm day!

JOE—(*To* MYRA)—Oh, get me a tumbler! I'll have some of it, if I have to steal it. Oh, I *will* have some.

[*Making a great noise till he finds a tumbler. A knock at the door.*]

Enter HENRY *and* MARTIN, *bearing a glass jar, containing what seems to be ice.*

JOE—(*Hurrying up to them*)—Oh, I am glad you've brought me some ice, for I am almost melted. Here is a glass; give me a drink at once. (*With much importunity.*)

HENRY—(*Carrying the jar*)—Why, Joe, it wont be of any use—

MARTIN—(*With a peculiar wink to* HENRY *and* MYRA, *which they at once understand*)—Yes, you shall have some. Bring on your tumbler. But you want some water in it first, and then I will put in a piece *all for yourself.*

HENRY—Yes, Joe, if you want some go and fill your tumbler with water. How warm the fellow is. See how the sweat rolls down his face.

(JOE *goes out for some water.*)

MARTIN—(*Softly*)—Keep on a sober face and we will have some fun with Joe, for I suppose he has been having one of his *tantrums.*

MYRA—Indeed he has! He declares he is going to melt, and I don't see as we can ever break him of his extravagant freaks.

Enter Joe.

Henry—Hullo! Here he comes with his glass brimming full. O Joe, wont you have a treat now? Poor fellow, to suffer so much from the heat, and then be laughed at us, no doubt, you have been by Myra!

Myra—I think if you had been here a few moments ago you would have laughed.

Martin—Come, my brave boy, put your tumbler on the table and I will drop in some pieces.

Joe—Oh, do hurry, for I can hardly wait.

Myra—Joe, why don't you set down the tumbler on the table? (*Taking hold of his hand.*) Pray don't act so foolish before folks!

Joe—Do get away, you little torment, for I can manage this drink myself. (*Pushing her away.*)

Martin—(*To* Joe)—Yes, set it down and let it stand a moment, for it can't possibly cool so much water in a moment.

[*He sets it down, and* Martin *picks out a few pieces from his jar, and puts them into the tumbler, when* Joe *seizes it and takes a swallow.*]

Joe—Why, this isn't one particle cooler than it was before.

Henry—Well, didn't we tell you to let it stand to cool? Now let it alone for two or three minutes.

Joe—Oh, but I am so hot! Myra, get a spoon and stir it. (Myra *gets one and stirs the water.*)

Martin—It will soon be ready. Don't you see; some of it is melting already!

Joe—Yes; but some of it don't melt at all.

Martin—Oh, well, that that don't melt is frozen a great deal harder than the other. It is singular how hard some things freeze.

(*Winking to* Myra *and* Henry.)

Joe—Well, let me have it now, I can't wait.

(*Seizes the tumbler and drains it off at one draught.*)

Henry—(*Springing to him quickly*)—Don't drink so much at once!

Joe—Oh, murder! What is it? What is it? It isn't ice; it isn't cold! Oh, murder, murder, how it burns my mouth! Is it poison—say quick!

(*Runs around with a wry face.*)

Martin—Don't you like it, Joe? Isn't it good this hot weather?

Joe—It's poison, it's poison; I am dying, I am dying!

Myra—Boys, what is it? (*Excitedly.*) Pray, what is it?

Henry—Don't you know what it is, Joe?

Joe—Oh, it's poison, it's poison!

Henry—Don't you know what it is?

Myra—Oh, boys! I am afraid it *is* poison! See how he raves, he is almost distracted. Hadn't we better send for a doctor?

Henry—Say, Joe, don't you *know* what it is?

Joe—No. But I know well enough it's poison.

Martin—Well, if you didn't know what it was, why were you so anxious to drink it? That is what I should like to know.

Joe—Oh, it's poison! You've poisoned me to death! I know I shall die.

Martin—No, you wont die either; but what did you want to drink it for if you didn't know what it was?

Joe—(*Calming himself a little*)—I thought it was ice.

Henry—Well, that didn't make it so, did it?

Myra—You say it isn't poison; pray what is it?

Joe—(*Brightening up still more, but spitting copiously*)—Yes, do tell what it is.

Martin—(*To Joe*)—You say it is poison; if it is, that settles the matter, and probably it will kill you.

Joe—Do tell me quick, is it poison?

Henry—Did you ever taste anything like it?

Joe—(*Puckering his mouth as if trying to discover what it is*)—I should think it was alum.

Henry—I guess it does pucker a little like alum, for it has the same nature, inasmuch as it *is* alum.

Martin—Yes, it is only alum, and a very fine specimen of quartz rock and glass for our museum. So cheer up, for it will not kill you just yet; neither do I think it will quench your thirst to any great extent.

Joe—But what did you say it was ice for when it was not?

Martin—We never said it was! You commenced furiously on us as we came in to show them to you, saying you were going to have some of that ice, and of course our generosity could not refuse you if we could do you any service. It is all your own fault, arising from your own greediness.

Joe—(*Hanging his head thoughtfully*)—I guess you are right. (*To the audience.*) It was the celebrated Dr. Franklin who said: "Never drink anything without seeing it; never sign anything without reading it," and I am now pretty well convinced from experimental knowledge, that Benjamin Franklin was a *wise man*; and further, that if the old saying, that "Experience is the best schoolmaster," is true, I shall endeavor to be wiser myself in the future than I have been in the past.

[*Curtain.*]

SAVED.

CHARACTERS:—PHILLIPS, Barkeeper.
PETERS, Drunkard.
BLANCHE, Drunkard's child.
BOLT, Jailer.
POLICEMAN NO. 1.
POLICEMAN NO. 2.
FAITH,
HOPE, } Three young Ladies.
CHARITY,

COSTUMES.—FAITH, HOPE and CHARITY should be dressed in white; hair long and loose over their shoulders, a band of white for coronet, with a gold or silver star at the forehead, a red sash passing over one shoulder and under the other arm, with the respective names upon them. PETERS and BLANCHE in ragged clothes. Others as fancy dictates.

NOTE.—Between the scenes, while the child is singing behind the curtain, the stage may be cleared for the next scene. If spoken in the evening, the stage should be dimly lighted in the second scene, only one distant light, and that above the speakers' heads, to represent the moon.

SCENE I.—A bar-room.

Enter man half drunk, begging for more drink.

PETERS—T-t-there's no use talking, landlord, I m-must have just one more drink.

PHILLIPS—Show me your money.

PETERS—D-did n't I say I haint g-got a red cent to my name?

PHILLIPS—Then don't come round me, begging, you poor drunken loafer; make yourself off, or I'll—

PETERS—D-d-do n't you call me a loafer, or I'll give you a dose of that. (*Shaking his fist.*) I'm just as good as you, the best day you ever see.

PHILLIPS—Come, come, don't shake you fists around here, I don't want to fight. You had better go and earn a sixpence somewhere, then come and ask for a drink, instead of standing here, begging away the hard earnings of respectable men.

PETERS—(*Straightening up and speaking quite soberly*)—Respectable men! Landlord, I aint a fool, if I be drunk. I wonder if you call your money hard-earned, when you stand here behind your counter, and take the last shinplaster from the hands of a hundred wretched drunkards like myself? I s'pose you think you are mighty respectable, because you can wear a paper collar and good clothes. Landlord, I was once just as respectable looking as you, but you've made me what I am. You've got my last sixpence, and now you tell me to go and earn another, to give to you. (*Turning round and speaking to himself.*) My poor, poor children, I wish I could stop, for your sakes; but I can't; it's no use.

PHILLIPS—No more of your blarney. Get out, I say!

PETERS—Not a step without a drink; I *must* have it!

PHILLIPS — Well, you wont, you know. (*Starting toward him.*) I've heard enough of your lip for one day. Go! You wont get a drink here!

PETERS—(*Advances a step and draws a pistol*)—Take care! don't you touch me, sir! I've come prepared for you to-day; you've got my last cent, now a drink or your life!

PHILLIPS—(*Runs behind counter*)—Murder!

Enter POLICEMAN No. 1. PETERS *discharges the pistol at him, but misses. Enter* POLICEMAN No. 2, *from behind, and seizes him.*

POLICEMAN No. 2—Not a very good marksman, but you're caught in the act, and now you may go with us. Give me your firearms.

[PETERS *struggles, but the pistol is wrenched from his hand by* POLICEMAN No. 1, *and he is led, still struggling, from the stage, followed by* PHILLIPS, *who is assisting the Policemen.*]

PHILLIPS—(*Walks slowly back, soliloquizing*)—Well, it's more luck than wit that I'm alive! Supposing that scoundrel had shot me. It's lucky that the police were so near at hand; but I declare, he's desperate. I'm glad he is in safe keeping; there's no knowing what he might do if he's allowed to run loose. (*Seats himself in a chair, places his feet on the top of a whiskey-barrel, tips his hat to one side of his head, and takes up a newspaper. While he is reading a child enters; he looks up and says:*) There comes one of his brats now. I was in hopes I had got rid of the whole crew, but they needn't come here, sniveling and begging. Zounds! she looks rough, though. I do feel kind o' sorry for her, anyhow.

Enter BLANCHE, *who walks up before him, and sings.*

BLANCHE—Please, Mr. Barkeeper, has father been here?
    He's not been at home for the day,
  'T is now almost midnight, and mother's in fear
    Some accident keeps him away.

PHILLIPS—(*Sings*)—No, no, little stranger; or yes, he's been here,
    Some officers took him away,
  He's gone to the lock-up, I'm sorry, my dear,
    He's done something wicked, they say.

BLANCHE—(*Sings*)—Oh! 't was not my father, who did the bad deed,
    'T was drinking that maddened his brain,
  Oh! let him go home to dear mother, I plead,
    I'm sure he'll not touch it again!
    (*Curtain falls and* BLANCHE *sings again :*)

BLANCHE—Please, Mister Policeman, my father is lost,
    A man says you took him away,
  Oh! can't he go home, sir; and what will it cost,
    If mother will send you the pay?

POLICEMAN NO. 1—(*Sings*)—Oh, no, little pleader, your father can't go!
We put him in prison, to-day,
Go home to your mother, and quick let her know,
What's keeping your father away.

BLANCHE—(*Sings*)—Oh! 't was not my father, etc.

[*Curtain.*]

SCENE II.—BOLT, the Jailer, armed, walking slowly back and forth across the stage.

Enter BLANCHE.

BLANCHE—(*Sings*)—Please, sir, Mister Jailer, please let me go in,
They say that my father's inside,
I scarcely can tell how unhappy we've been,
We could not feel worse, had he died.
Please, sir, it was drinking that made him do wrong,
I'm sure, sir, he will drink no more,
Oh, just a few minutes, a minute's not long,—
But no one will open the door.
(*Turns to go away, singing low and mournfully.*)
Oh! 't was not my father, etc.

[BOLT *takes a seat at the door where the prison is supposed to be.*]

Enter FAITH, HOPE *and* CHARITY *from different parts of the stage. They join hands.*

CHARITY—Welcome, sweet sisters, my helpers in every good and noble work. We've met again on a mission of love. What shall we do first to best promote our object?

HOPE—We'll hope and pray.

FAITH—We'll trust in God.

CHARITY—Heaven help us, then; thou, sweet Hope, shall be my guiding star; and thou, dear Faith, my anchor; and mine shall be the hand to lift our fallen brother, and save him from ruin; let us go. (*They advance toward* BOLT, *and* CHARITY *hands him a paper.*) Mr. Jailer, here is a letter of pardon from the authorities, will you release our brother?

BOLT—(*Reads it, and then says*)—Can it be possible, that the wretched vagabond, shut up in this dungeon, is your brother?

CHARITY—We are sisters to all mankind. There is none so low as to be beneath our notice, and none so degraded as to deserve our scorn. When a poor, erring mortal has advanced far down the broad road to ruin, and a world joins its forces to dash him over the brink of destruction, then it is our mission to win him back, set him on an equal footing with us, and teach him the way to Heaven.

BOLT—Yours is a good mission, friends; you have my best wishes for your success. Wait here, and I will bring the prisoner.

[*Goes and brings the prisoner with him, dragging his chains.*]

CHARITY—Loose him, and let him go.

BOLT—(*Looses him, and says*)—There, go! you're free again, thanks to the efforts of these friends, in your behalf. May you be a better man for their sake, and the sake of your family.   (*Throws off the chains.*)

PETERS—How can I ever thank you for your kindness, my unknown benefactors?

FAITH—Not so unknown as you suppose. Our good sister, Charity, has been a frequent visitor to your wretched home.

PETERS—Don't speak of my home, I beg of you. (*Sits down and leans his head in his hands, speaking remorsefully.*) I had a home once, and love and respect; but I have none now; and rum has been my ruin. I had friends once, but I have none now; nobody to help me reform, if I wished.

Hope—Do you remember, when poor trusting Faith and trembling Hope were thrust outside your doors?

Peters—Yes, yes, I remember! My poor wife and children, how they have suffered.

Charity—Yes, brother, they have suffered, and even now they are weeping for you, hoping, trusting that you will yet be an honor to yourself and them.

Peters—I can not! that never can be! I'm disgraced and ruined! I'm driven from good society, and shunned by everybody. No, no! it's too late now! (*Speaks impatiently.*) Leave me alone, there's no use, I'm a lost man!

Charity — (*Advances, and lays her hand upon his shoulder*)—Brother, don't talk thus, I pray you. I know the world is harsh; temptation will follow you, slander will assail you, pride and malice will trample upon you, society will shun you; but don't say you have *no* friends. Look up, and behold the three angels, who will ever attend you in your hours of darkest trials.

Peters—(*Looks up, hastily*)—Faith! Hope! Charity! but the greatest of these is Charity. Are these, then, my friends, these, angels in disguise? (*Takes an empty bottle from his pocket, holds it up, and looks at it; talking as if addressing it.*) I had thought that this was all the friend I had; but, instead of a friend, thou hast been but the lurking-place of a demon. Never again shalt thou deceive me. What care I now for your temptations! I have friends, true friends, the angels of Faith, Hope, and Charity; and they have saved me. (*Rises quickly, dashes the bottle upon the floor, crushing it to pieces, and shouts loudly:*) Saved, saved at last!

[*Curtain.*]

SCENE III.—Tableau.—PETERS reformed.

The back part of the stage should be hidden from the audience, by a curtain which opens in the center. This can easily be arranged according to taste or convenience. Upon the rising of the curtain, FAITH and CHARITY are discovered to the right and left of the central opening of the curtain, a few feet from each other, with their right and left arms extended and grasping the curtain, as if about to draw it apart and open. HOPE is discovered a few feet in advance, and midway between them, with the fore-finger of her right hand to her lips, as if invoking silence. While "*Home, Sweet Home*" is played or sung, very softly, in the distance, HOPE slowly moves her finger from her lips, and points to the scene which is being revealed, as FAITH and CHARITY gradually draw the curtain open, disclosing PETERS, his wife and BLANCHE seated around the supper-table, PETERS in the act of asking a blessing upon the meal.

[*Curtain.*]

TWO WAYS OF TELLING THE SAME THING.

CHARACTERS:—FRED SCOTT, } two Boys.
NED SNOOSY,

SCENE.—A platform. FRED SCOTT steps out as if to make a speech.

FRED—I want to tell you all about the walk I took with Ned,
While all you lazy people here were sound asleep in bed.
I woke before 'twas hardly light, and quickly rose and dressed,
The day was breaking in the East, the moon shone in the West.

I called to Ned; called once, called twice, before he
    scrambled down,
And soon we two with hurrying steps had left the dozing
    town.
And then I saw a splendid sight! The East was all
    aglow,
With pink-edged purple clouds, and streaks of blue and
    gold below.
And then the sun arose, a great and glowing ball of red,
From out a heap of crimson clouds, like cushions of a
    bed;
He gleamed across the sky, the earth was flushed with
    ruddy light,
On every leaf and blade of grass were diamonds flashing
    bright.
Long shadows stretched along the ground, each leaf in
    quivering play,
And sunlight warmed and lighted up where all was cold
    and grey.
I see you smile at my big words; I say you needn't
    laugh,
For of the splendid sight I saw, I have not told you
    half.

  NED—(*Calls out from the audience*)—I don't believe
    your yarn!

  FRED—You don't, you ugly, grinning elf!
Just you get up here on the stage and tell the thing
    yourself!

           Enter NED.

  NED—Look here, what's that you're going on about,
    you stupid fellow?
The sun was bright, the shadows long, the sky was red
    and yellow?

Well, what of it? A patch of red is no such wondrous sight
That just to see it one should wake in the middle of the night. (*To the audience.*)
I'm out of patience with this goose, (I will not call him fool,
Because, I'm sorry to confess, he stands ahead at school,)
But then he has such curious ways I can not well make out,
I did not see such splendid things to gabble so about.
I saw the sun rise, too, this morning. What of that? I dare
To say 't would have risen all the same if I had not been there.
To tell the truth, it was so early I could hardly keep -
My eyes from shutting up, and I was almost half asleep.
And then the air was damp and chilly; one might know 't would be
At such an early hour, and I was shivering dreadfully.
And then those diamonds bright of his—those penetrating dews,
Had wet my trowsers to my knees, and soaked quite through my shoes.
Now I have this advice to give: I pray you all take warning,
And never be caught out of bed on such a wretched morning.

FRED—O Ned!

NED—Yes, Fred,
It *was* a wretched morning, those are the words I said;
I'll stick to them, and call them true, though you should kill me dead.

So where's the use of quarreling? You see we can't
    agree.   (*In unison.*)

{ NED—It was a wretched morning as ever I did see.
{ FRED—It was a splendid morning as ever I did see.

                                (*To the audience.*)

Now if this fellow hadn't stopped me with his foolish
    talk,
I would have told you more about our very pleasant walk.
The roosters crowing near and far replied to one another,
And here and there we came across a careful old hen
    mother,
Who clucked and scratched for her young brood thus
    early in the morn,
And in a field we saw some ducks nip off the growing
    corn.
The men came out to feed their stock, the maids to milk
    the cows.
We watched the blue smoke curling up from out each
    wayside house.
Oh, all the world was waking up—each pig, and colt and
    calf,
I wanted just to run, and hop, and jump, and sing and
    laugh,
Turn summersaults, and fences climb; but Ned here was
    so lazy—

  NED—So *tired* you mean! *You* was so brisk you
    almost set me crazy.
You know I was so tired I scarce could drag myself
    along,
And still you wanted me to run, and climb, and sing a
    song;
Or else you wanted me to stay and see an ugly daisy,
Or watch a stupid bumble-bee a humming round a flower.

Although I begged you hard to stop and rest for half an
    hour.
I never saw a boy so wild about the birds and things,
As though *I* knew or cared what kind of song a cat-
    bird sings!
I only know I saw one sitting on a fence we passed,
And I thought, "Now there's a chance for a little fun at
    last."
And so I stopped and found a stone at the ugly bird to
    fling,
In hopes, if I could not kill it quite, perhaps I'd break its
    wing;
But then it up and flew away, the good-for-nothing thing!
Then you wanted even to see a rose, 'twas such a pretty
    blue—

    FRED—O Ned!

    NED—'Tis true!

    FRED—'T was red.

    NED—'T was blue,
But as for that I do not care! I'm sure I never knew
Whether a rose was red or white or black or green or
    blue.
You see I'm not so great a goose about a flower as you!

    FRED—(*To the audience*)—You hear him! Did you
    ever know a boy that so lacked sense?
He says he tried to kill a bird that sat upon the fence.
I know he caught the butterflies and pinned them on his
    hat,
And kicked a little dog, and tried to set him on a cat.
But still we had a splendid time—

    NED—   Speak for yourself, I pray!

FRED—I gathered all the flowers I found in fields
    along our way,
You never saw such pretty flowers—

NED—   I never will again
If I must rise at four o'clock to see them; that is plain!

FRED—I filled a bottle full of bugs with green and
    golden wings—

NED—(*To the audience*)—I never saw a boy so wild
    about his bugs and things!
There's one thing that I soon found out; that is, that
    bees have stings.
You see, I tried—

FRED—(*To the audience*)—He caught a bee and shut
    it in a flower,
And kept it close there buzzing loud for nearly half an
    hour;
But when he tried to look at it, the poor thing got away,
And buzzing round, it made him for his cruel cunning
    pay.
It stung his hand—

NED—   The mean old thing! I feel it smarting yet,
When I can catch another bee, that sting I sha'n't forget.

FRED—(*To the audience*)—But then I haven't told
    you half the pleasure that I found;
I saw a buzzard in the sky go sailing round and round.
I saw the crows go cawing past, a thousand crows or more;
I'm sure I never saw so many crows at once before.
A hundred birds sang in the trees, each one a different
    tune;
The nicest time in all the year is just this month of June!

We found some berries hidden in the grass, so nice and
    red,
We stopped to pick and eat them—

N<small>ED</small>—   Tell the whole now, Master Fred,
How as I tried to climb the fence my pantaloons I tore,
And there you stood and laughed, while I—

F<small>RED</small>—You tugged and almost swore,
And every time I think of it I have to laugh the more.

N<small>ED</small>—And then what were the berries worth, so small,
    unripe and sour!
And I so hungry, too, because 't was past the breakfast
    hour!

F<small>RED</small>—(*To the audience*)—I found a bird's nest in a
    bush! Oh, such a cunning sight!
It had four little eggs in it, all speckled brown and white.
I called to Ned to come and see, and then—what will you
    say?
He wanted to destroy the nest and take the eggs away!
And then—why—I—

N<small>ED</small>—   You need n't brag, you bully! If I let
You whip me once, it doesn't mean I shall not pay you
    yet,
When I am not so sleepy quite; I shall not let it pass;
I can whip you any day I try, if you *are* first in the class.

F<small>RED</small>—We'll see, young man! (*To the audience.*)
    I haven't time to tell you any more,
For I'm so hungry I can scarcely stand upon the floor.
I've not had breakfast yet; I say, I think there's nothing
    quite
So good as a morning walk to give a boy an appetite.

NED—O dear! I'm tired out, I'm not so big a dunce as Fred;
And when I get my breakfast done I'm going back to bed. [*Exit* NED.

FRED—Well, let him go, and yawn and snooze. I *wont* be called a fool,
And when I get *my* breakfast done, I'm going straight to school.

[*Curtain.*]

AUNT DEBBY'S SPECULATION.

CHARACTERS:—AUNT DEBBY PINCHUM.
TOM, the hired Man.
OLIVE, Aunt Debby's Niece.
KEENE, a Swindler.

SCENE I.—AUNT DEBBY'S sitting-room. AUNT DEBBY seated knitting.

Enter TOM.

TOM—Here's the price for them 'ere chickens, marm, twenty-two cents a pound, just seventy-three pounds, comes to sixteen dollars and six cents.

AUNT DEBBY—(*Clutching the money*)—Dear me, Tom, couldn't you have got another cent a pound, by trying hard? 'pears to me men are mighty shiftless now-a-days. Now, when I druv to market in my younger days, nobody could get the start of me in prices.

TOM—I guess it was a high day, Miss Pinchum, when you got ten cents a pound for your poultry. Now it's twenty-two, and you want twenty-three. Folks are never satisfied.

AUNT DEBBY—But consider how living has gone up, just look at the price of chickens' feed.

Tom—(*Muttering to himself as he goes out*)—Livin' hasn't ris much in this place, as my stomach can testify. I declare I wont stay to be starved out in this style.

(*Goes out.*)

Aunt Debby—(*Counting her money*)—Well, this isn't so bad. It is a dollar and forty-six cents more than I expected. (*Starting suddenly.*) Oh, that thief! (*Runs to the door and screams:*) Tom, Tom!

Enter Tom.

Tom—Well, now, what's to pay? One would think the house was a-fire.

Aunt Debby—Where's that six cents?

Tom—Well now I did forget that. (*Draws out an old leathern wallet.*) Here it is, and much good may it do you.

[*Exit* Tom.

[Aunt Debby *goes to a box in the corner, and takes out an old black stocking. She seats herself, takes out a roll of bills, and pours some silver pieces in her lap.*]

Aunt Debby—Twenty-five, fifty, seventy-five, one hundred. All as good as gold. It's time to send these down to the bank-safe along with the rest, but it's such a comfort to have a little by a body.

(*Chinks the silver pieces and smiles.*)

Enter Olive. Aunt Debby *throws her apron over the money.*

Olive—Oh, don't mind me, Aunt Debby. I sha'n't steal, if I do want some money pretty bad.

Aunt Debby—(*Peevishly*)—Oh, yes, I dare say, there's something you are a wanting now. It's just money, money all the time.

Olive—But how can I study, Aunt Debby, without books? I've borrowed and borrowed until I am ashamed of myself. I must have a new History now, or give up the study. I shall never be prepared for a teacher at this rate.

Aunt Debby—Well, I do think, of all schools I ever heard of, yours is the most expensivest. It's just expense upon expense, new books and new fol-da-rols all the time. Now when I went to school we was well off with our spellin' books and English Readers and samplers, and a skein of blue cotton thread to work with. Them girls that had a skein of red and green sewing silk besides, were counted rich.

Olive—Well, times have changed, auntie. They never ask for our samplers now, when we apply for a school. But will you not let me have the dollar for the History out of that lapful of money I saw you counting when I came in?

Aunt Debby—(*Gathering her apron a little closer*)— You must think of my expenses, child. Just see what it costs to keep up this place. Look at the price of chickens' feed, and see how much that ungrateful Tom eats every time he sits down to the table. It's enough to break a bank.

Olive—But see what the place brings you in, auntie, and how valuable Tom is to you. I shouldn't wonder if he didn't stay long, unless you give him better fare. But about the book, auntie, do please now get it for me; just see how I patch and save my dresses so as to help to get an education.

Aunt Debby—Will you go without butter till you pay me back?

Olive—I will as soon as I can have coffee again. But I can't well do without both, as bread and water would be dry living for breakfast and supper. Let's see; I have gone without coffee for two weeks now. I believe you called it two cents a day. That makes twenty-eight cents. It will take me three weeks more to pay for in Algebra. Then I will begin on the butter. But it is a hard way to get an education to starve one's self into it.

AUNT DEBBY—I'll risk its hurting you any, to go without butter and coffee. They aint good for young folks. There's nothing better for them than good plain mush and skimmed milk, and it's all foolishness in you to say you can't eat it. You'd like it well enough if you'd try it steady for a spell. Well, I suppose I shan't have a minute's peace until that book is got, so take your dollar and be off, but mind you've got to pay me back every cent. And now don't you let me hear another word about money again this year.

(*Gives her a dollar, gathers up her apron and goes out.*)

OLIVE—I *could not* thank her, glad as I am to get the book. Oh, what a wretched way to live! How can I bear it? How bitter to be dependent. But courage for only one year more, then I hope to be free from such fetters. [*Exit* OLIVE.

[*Curtain.*]

SCENE II.—AUNT DEBBY, spectacles on, seated at a table, reading a letter; various papers scattered over it.

AUNT DEBBY—Well, this beats all creation. I never saw nor heard of this chap, who signs himself St. John A. Goldsmith; but here he writes me a letter saying I have drawn a prize of a thousand dollars, in a lottery away off in Kentucky. He says I musn't tell anybody about it. But I must send him fifty dollars to get five hundred of my prize money, or a hundred dollars to get the whole thousand. I can't just see through it, but as far as I can learn the hundred dollars pays for my ticket, which is but reasonable when they pay you back a thousand. I have often thought what an easy way it was to make money, and here it comes right to my door. I've a great mind to tell Olive. She'd never tell, I know, and she could write my letter for me, she's such a good penman. (*Steps to the door and calls:*) Olive, Olive!

OLIVE—(*Entering hastily, her sleeves rolled up*)—What is it, auntie? You look excited. **Has** anything happened?

AUNT DEBBY—Jest sit down, Olive, and read that letter and them papers, and tell me what you think of them.

[OLIVE *reads. The old lady rubs her glasses, and watches her intently.*]

OLIVE—It's a precious mess of nonsense, auntie, and you would never see your money again if you were foolish enough to send it. Just look at the morals of the man. He directs you to date your letter a month back, and says he will alter the post-mark to correspond, so as to deceive the "Board of Trustees." Now if he would deceive them, do you think he would hesitate much to deceive you? Depend upon it, he is the "Board" himself, unless he has an accomplice or two in his swindling operations. I have often heard of such things before. So I beg of you, auntie, don't have any thing to do with it. I must make up my corn bread now; and if you say so, I will light my fire with these papers.

AUNT DEBBY—No, no; I will save them for something else. One side is good white paper. (*Exit* OLIVE.) Now that is the most tantalizing girl I ever seen in my life. Here she must come in and spoil all my pretty calculations. But never mind; I'll write the man a letter myself, and just ask if he is *certain sure* that there's no mistake about it, and that I'll surely get my money, and if it is all right I'll send, no matter what Olive says. I'll just write to-night, and send it off in the evening-mail.

It will go to New York to-night, and he can answer by to-morrow, if he has a mind to. I wont tell Olive a word though, about it. So I must write quick while she is getting supper. (*Takes down pen, ink, and paper, and writes, folds and directs the letter.*) Now I'll just slip out to the post-office, and if Olive asks me where I've been, I'll tell her I went to the store for a skein of thread. [*Exit.*

[*Curtain.*]

Scene III.—Aunt Debby, seated, knitting.

Aunt Debby—I was so disappointed, not to get a letter to-day; but I think it will certainly come to-morrow. Maybe he was 'fronted 'cause I didn't send along the money at first, and wont have nothing more to do with me. It's all that girl's fault. I should never have thought of misdoubting him, if she hadn't put me up to it. (*Rap at the door.*) Massy sakes! who is that knocking at the door? (*Opens the door.*)

[*Enter* Keene, *heavy whiskers, very dignified, solemn manner.*]

Aunt Debby—(*Courtesying*)—Will you walk in, sir?

Keene—(*Bowing low, hat in hand*)—Thank you, madam. (*Walks in,* Aunt Debby *giving him a seat.*) You are probably surprised, my dear madam, at seeing a stranger in your house; but as I was passing through your beautiful village, I thought I would call on you a few moments. My name is St. John A. Goldsmith. (*Bowing and smiling.*) I believe it is not quite unfamiliar to you.

Aunt Debby—Land sakes! who'd 've thought it! Excuse me, Mr. Goldsmith, but you have put me quite in a flutter.

Keene—No occasion for it at all, my dear madam; I thought you hardly understood the matter with regard to which I addressed you; and since I was riding along in the cars, it has occurred to me that you would take more interest in a mining company I am interested in than in the lottery. I think you mentioned you were alone, no man to manage your affairs. Your husband is dead, I suppose? *(Bowing respectfully.)*

Aunt Debby—*(Simpering)*—Ahem—no, sir,—I—ahem, I never married.

Keene—Indeed! I am very much surprised. I mistook you for a young widow. But never mind my blunders. I am a very blundering man, at the best. As I was saying, you can dispose of your property as you see fit, having no one to *dictate* to you; and this mining company declares a dividend of fifty per cent. a month. Just imagine how a few hundreds, or thousands, would double themselves, over and over, every year, in that company. And all you have to do, is to take stock in it. You do not have to turn your hand to work. You could soon be the richest lady in the land, and ride in a golden coach, with gold-mounted harness on your horses. You might build you a palace which would be the pride of the whole country. The shares, as you will see by the prospectus, are fifty dollars each. The capital of the company is four millions; so you see you are perfectly secure, *perfectly.* Now, if you would like to invest a little in this, I am willing to serve you. Indeed, I shall be *happy* to do so, though I am exceedingly hurried and pressed with business, and seldom stop in such small towns. Indeed, I may say, I called this evening expressly to accommodate you; and my time is very precious, very, indeed.

(Looks at his watch.)

Aunt Debby—I am sure I am very much obliged to

you; but the thing is so sudden-like; couldn't you give me a little time to think about it, and talk with my friends?

KEENE—(*Buttoning his coat, with an offended air*)—I fear I have been deceived in you, madam; and I will not trouble you further. (*Picks up his hat.*) What I have said has been in the strictest confidence, and from a sincere desire to serve you. I might lose my position as Director, if it should be known; and as you decline my offer, I can only beg you will not mention it.

(*Arises, as if to go.*)

AUNT DEBBY—(*Much agitated*)—But I didn't say I declined. Please, Mr. Goldsmith, take a chair again; I didn't pertend to say I wouldn't invest; I only wanted to think over it. (KEENE *takes his seat, still holding his hat.*) But if you think there's no mistake, I don't mind putting in a little in the business. There's about four hundred in the bank, and I have another hundred and odd about me. Now, would you advise me to put in all, or only half?

KEENE—(*Brightening up*)—My dear madam, put in only half, if you see fit; but *mark my words*, you'll be sorry you didn't put in the whole, when your dividends come piling in so fast every month.

AUNT DEBBY—Well, Mr. Goldsmith, would you mind waiting here a few minutes, till I get my money? It's after bank hours, but Mr. Edmonds is my neighbor, and I know he'll oblige me. It is only a step over there.

KEENE—Certainly, certainly, madam, only be sure and remember my caution about mentioning this matter to any one, or I drop the whole concern.

AUNT DEBBY—Certain, certain; I sha'n't be gone but a minute. [*Exit.*

KEENE—(*Getting up and going to a drawer*)—I wonder what the old girl has stowed away here. Two silver spoons, as sure as I live! Here they go into the silver-mine. (*Drops them into his pocket, chuckling and laughing softly.*) These pocket handkerchiefs will be useful; they may follow. What a mean old thing she must be! Her bureaus are absolutely not worth picking? I wish I could take a peep into the rest of her house. But I must take my seat, and draw on my professional face again.

[*Seats himself, and spreads out a number of maps and papers on the table.*]

Enter AUNT DEBBY.

AUNT DEBBY—Here I am, at last; Mr. Edmonds asked me a good many questions, but I put him off every time. So he don't suspect nothing.

KEENE—(*In some alarm*)—How far off does he live?

AUNT DEBBY—Oh, just down the street. It's well I went just as I did, for he was just starting for Centerville, ten miles away, to be there early to court in the morning. They've got a batch of counterfeiters to try, and he has to be there to prove something or other. Ain't you well, Mr. Goldsmith, you look so queer somehow?

KEENE—Perfectly well, perfectly, madam; I have sometimes a trifling dizziness in my head; but it soon passes over. Now, let us proceed to business at once. I have made out your certificate of stock, five hundred dollars' worth. There you have it. Now I will affix a stamp, and it will be all legal. Here is my address in New York; and here are the cards of the company. I will leave several with you; and any time you are in the city, just call. We are always glad to see the stockholders, and to give them all the information in our power. If you have counted the money, it is not necessary for me to do so; I have perfect confidence in your honesty, perfect.

[*Bows and smiles as he receives the roll of bills from her hand, and exits hastily.*]

AUNT DEBBY—(*Gathering up her papers*)—Now, I must keep these, choice as gold, and hide them from Olive. I know she wouldn't approve of it; but I guess she'll think differently, when I get my first dividends. I shall get half my money back in thirty days. It's a sight easier than raising chickens. [*Exit.*

[*Curtain.*]

SCENE IV.—OLIVE, dusting the sitting-room.

Enter TOM.

TOM—Is the mistress any better this morning, Miss Olive?

OLIVE—No better, Tom, and the doctor hardly thinks she ever will be. She seems quiet, and comfortable, though; and that's a blessing, after the stormy time we have had. But the shock has completely broken her. She talks about her silver-mine, when she says any thing; and has quite forgotten, that she was swindled out of all her money. She seems to be looking for great returns every day. She sometimes counts the checks on the counterpane, and thinks they are silver pieces. Uncle Henry will stay a few days, and set things to rights; and he would like you to stay on, and manage affairs just as you have; and he will make a fair bargain with you, Tom.

TOM—(*Fumbling his hat*)—If you please, miss, I would like to speak a word with you, about some help for the kitchen. It would never do for you to take all the care of the old lady and the housekeeping too.

OLIVE—(*Smiling*)—So you think Mary Jane would be

a good assistant, do you? Well, bring her here as soon as you like. I have already spoken to Uncle Henry about it, and he approves of it highly.

Tom—(*Glowing with smiles*)—Bless you, Miss Olive, I'll serve you to the end of my days.   [*Exit.*

Olive—And this is the end of my poor aunt's dream of wealth. How terrible it seems, to see her so broken. I am sorry, now, for my many impatient words and thoughts toward her; but she shall not want for any care and attention I can give, while her life lasts. There, I hear her calling now.

(*Lays by her duster, and hastily exits.*
[*Curtain.*]

ILLINOIS.*

AN ACTING CHARADE.

CHARACTERS:—Husband.
Wife.
Boy.

Scene.—Wife, discovered sewing.

Enter Husband.

Husband—(*With hand over his eye, groaning*)—Oh dear! oh dear! oh dear!

Wife—(*Rushing to him*)—What is it, husband! Are you ill?

Husband—Yes. Oh dear! oh!

Enter Boy, *making great noise.*

Wife—(*To* Boy)—Hush-sh-sh-sh! Your father is *ill*. He's hurt his *eye*. Stop that *noise!*

(*Helps out* Husband, *followed by* Boy.)
[*Curtain.*]

---

* In "Illinois," sound the final "s."

THE YOUNG DEBATERS.

CHARACTERS:—THOMAS JONES, large Boy.
HARRY LEE,
FRANK HART,   } small Boys.
BENNIE NELSON,
ALBERT WAYNE,

SCENE.—A school-room, or an apartment in a house.

THOMAS—Didn't you little fellows say you wanted to learn to debate?

HARRY, FRANK, BENNIE and ALBERT—(*Shouting*)— Yes, yes! oh, yes! We do! That's it! Let's debate! debate!

THOMAS—Come here, then, and we will arrange matters. What question would you like to debate?

HARRY—I don't know; I never debated.

FRANK—I heard Ben Bingham talking about a horse and cow question.

THOMAS—Well, can you state the question?

FRANK—No, I never stated a question in my life.

THOMAS—Bennie, can you tell me what the horse and cow question is? Can you state it or tell it to me?

BENNIE—I think this is it: "Is a horse more useful than a cow?"

THOMAS—That's right! Well, will that question suit you?

ALBERT—I think I would like this question, "Is a dog more useful to a man than a gun?"

THOMAS—A very good question, indeed. What do you say, young Websters and Clays, will you take the dog and gun question?

ALL TOGETHER—I'm agreed! All right! It will suit us!

THOMAS—Who will take the affirmative and who the negative?

HARRY—I don't know what that means.

THOMAS—(*Laughs*)—Ha! ha! Well, I'll try to explain. Those who are on the affirmative will affirm, or say that a dog is more useful to a man than a gun, whilst those who are on the negative will deny that a dog is more useful to a man than a gun. Do you think you understand?

ALL—I do. And so do I.

ALBERT—I want to be on the gun side of the question.

THOMAS—That will be the negative. Who will assist Albert on the gun side?

BENNIE—I will, if you will let me; and I think we can whip the other boys all to pieces. Why, sir, a gun is a useful thing—it is a weapon—you can shoot with a gun—

THOMAS—Hold on, Mr. Debater, you are too fast. It isn't your time to speak. The affirmative must open the debate.

BENNIE—Oh, I thought you wanted me to go ahead. Well, I'll wait till the *firmament* talks.

THOMAS—(*Laughs*)—Ha! ha! What's the firmament?

BENNIE—Why, it is the dog side of the question.

THOMAS—Oh, yes! Well, Harry, you are on the *firmament*, as Bennie says; we will let you open the debate. You must make a speech and endeavor to show that a dog is more useful to a man than a gun. You can commence.

HARRY—(*Somewhat frightened*)—I don't know what to say.

THOMAS—Walk right out here and say something. Don't be frightened. Nobody will hurt you. You can say a few words, anyhow, but you must not speak more than five minutes.

HARRY—I don't think I can speak half a minute. Well, then, I think a dog is a very useful animal. He has four tails and one leg. (*Boys laugh.*) I mean he has four legs and one tail. He has a mouth and a nose, and his nose—that is—his nose is always cold—his nose is. Our dog—we have a dog—our dog is a setter, he sets 'most all the time. The name of our dog is Bingo; he was called after the dog in the song. The song says, "There was a butcher had a dog, and Bingo was his name."

THOMAS—I don't like to interrupt you; you are making a very good speech, but you ought to try to show that a dog is more useful to a man than a gun.

HARRY—I thought I was showing that. Well, I'll commence again. A dog is a very useful animal. He has four legs; two of his legs are hind legs and two of them are fore legs; the hind legs are stuck on behind and the fore legs are stuck on before. If a dog had no fore legs behind and no hind legs before he would not be so useful an animal. He would not be so useful because he could not run much. If he had no nose he would not be so useful either, for he smells with his nose. Most all dogs smell with the nose. He smells on the track, and he runs on it, and sometimes catches up to it. You would think, sometimes, to see a dog running on his track, that he would run over his nose, but he never does. A dog is useful to bark at night. He is useful to a man because he runs after him, and a gun does not. You have to put your gun on your shoulder before it will run after you.

THOMAS—Harry, your time is up. (*Harry sits down.*) Now, Bennie, you have a chance to talk on the gun side.

BENNIE—I was going to say before, that a gun was a **very useful animal**, and I'll stick to it.

Thomas—That is, you are going to stick to that which you were going to say before. Ah, yes, I understand.

Bennie—(*Speaking very loud*)—Yes, sir-ee! The gun is the most useful animal in the wilds of North America and Nova Scotia.

Thomas—Too loud for a little boy. Become calm before you proceed, or you will alarm the neighbors.

Bennie—How can I be calm when there is—when there is—that is—when there is—

Thomas—So much at issue. I understand; go ahead.

Bennie—Yes, sir! The gun is the most useful animal.

Thomas—You are not debating the question, "is the horse a more useful animal than the cow?" Please don't refer to the gun as an animal, it makes me nervous.

Bennie—It was only a mistake of the tongue. But, sir, the gun is the most useful an—that is, he is the most useful gun in the world. Where would we have been to-day if it hadn't been for the gun? As I said before, a gun will shoot. You can shoot with a gun, and you can not shoot with a dog. Where is the man that ever shot with a dog? If General George W. Washington had had no gun when he landed on Plymouth Rock in the Spring of 1776, where would we have been to-day? But he had a gun, and now we can all sit around our firesides and play checkers, or whistle "Yankee Doodle" and "Put me in My Little Bed." The gun is made by a gunsmith. Guns do not eat as much as dogs, and hence it follows that they are usefuler. Our dog is an awful eater. I think I have made it clear to you that the gun is the most useful an—most useful gun than a dog.

Thomas—Clear as mud, Bennie; but you have exhausted yourself, and may rest awhile. Frank, you are on the affirmative. You may reply to Bennie's spread eagle speech if you can reach it.

FRANK—I don't think I can say much, as I never debated before. But I think the dog is the most useful animal. I believe the question is, "Is a dog more useful to a gun than a man?"

THOMAS—(*Laughs*)—Ha! ha! You are badly shipwrecked. Do you wish to debate on the gun or on the dog side?

FRANK—You said I would be on the dog side.

THOMAS—All right; but your question is, "Is a dog more useful to a man than a gun?" Now, go ahead.

FRANK—I say it is. A dog is very useful to man, from the fact that he is a very useful animal. If we had no dogs how could we hunt rabbits? "A dog will bite a thief at night," and therefore, a dog is a very useful animal. A dog will drive the pigs out of the yard and the chickens out of the garden, therefore, a dog is a very useful animal. A dog will hunt wood-chucks and raccoons, and sometimes he will kill snakes, therefore, a dog is a very useful animal. The dog is also a noble animal, but men often abuse dogs, which isn't nice in man. I heard the other day of a shabby trick which a man played upon his dog. The man was in a great wood, he was far away from any house, and had nothing to eat. What did he do? Why he cut off the dog's tail, ate the meat off of it, and then gave the dog the bone. Now, that's what I call a shabby trick. But perhaps that saved the man's life. If the man had had a gun, where would he have been? If he had had a gun he could not have cut off the dog's tail. The tail was not there, neither was the dog there. He could not have cut off the gun's —that is, I mean—I mean, of course, the man would have been in a bad fix. If he had had a gun instead of a dog he might have perished there in the midst of that great howler of a wilderness. Guns are very good in their place, but they often go off unexpectedly, spreading famine and destruction around them.

Thomas—Famine and destruction—that's the idea. You'll make a debater some day, Frank. Now, Albert, you may come forward and fire on the gun side.

Albert—"He is fallen. We may now pause before that splendid prodigy which towered among us like some ancient ruin, whose power terrified the glance its magnificence attracted. Grand, gloomy and peculiar—"

Thomas—Halt! The name of Albert Wayne on this occasion stands upon the list of debaters, and not on the list of declaimers. I'd like to know what the "Character of Napoleon Bonaparte" has to do with the important question, "Is a dog more useful to a man than a gun?"

Albert—I know I am expected to debate the gun side of the question, but I never debated before, and I thought I could kind of get into the hang of the thing if I should first speak a few sentences of an old declamation.

Thomas—You will only be allowed five minutes, and if you consume your time in speaking declamations, you will not assist your "worthy colleague" very much.

Albert—Well, I'll make another attempt. The dog is—that is—I mean the gun is.—Guns are made in many places. Some guns are made by gunsmiths, and some are made by other persons. Pop-guns are not made by gunsmiths. The gun is useful—the gun—(*stammers*,) the gun. I find that debating is hard work, but I suppose it will be the making of me if I keep at it. This reminds me of a story brother Bob read the other day. I guess I can't tell it just the way it was in the paper, but I can tell it my own way. A good while ago when dog-fighting was more in vogue than it is at the present time, a young man who was raising a fighting pup, induced his old father to get down on all-fours and imitate the dog.

The pup caught the father by the nose and held on. The son disregarding the old gentleman's cries, exclaimed: "Hold him, Growler, hold him! Bear it, father, bear it; it will be the makin' of the pup." Guns are of various sizes. When there is a big war going on, a great many guns are made and a great many guns are thrown away; the soldiers throw them away when they want to run pretty fast. The last argument I have to offer, is this: An army of men carrying dogs would be of but little use, whilst an army of men carrying guns can shoot and make a noise. Where would the Revolutionary war have been to-day, if it hadn't been for guns? A dog is not of much account. Uncle Joe had a bad dog once, and he took him into a crowd and tried to lose him, but the dog was home before Uncle Joe.

THOMAS—Time's up, Albert.

ALBERT—I'm glad of that, for I didn't know what I would say next.

THOMAS—You have all done remarkably well for a first effort, and I hope you will keep at it. As Albert says, it may be hard work, but it will be the making of you if you persevere, and whenever you feel like debating again, I will take pleasure in listening to you.

[*Curtain.*]

THE TWO DOLLS.

FOR THE VERY LITTLE FOLKS.

CHARACTERS:—GEORGE, a little Merchant.
KITTY, CELIA, } two little Girls.
CAPTAIN HUTTON, Celia's Uncle.

SCENE I.—GEORGE, *seated behind a counter, on which are arranged boxes and toys.*

Enter KITTY, *a poorly-dressed little girl.*

KITTY—I want to buy a doll, a very pretty doll!

GEORGE—A rag doll, with good-shaped head, black ink eyebrows, pokeberry red cheeks, and red worsted lips—and with a beautiful dress of calico—we have a case of these, just from Paris.

[*He throws out a most absurd-looking little home-made doll.*]

KITTY—Oh, but it's pretty! O my! O dear! O goodness! O sakes! a real beauty! I'll get that, if I have enough money! Sakes alive, what a beauty! (*Turning it round and round.*) I must have this, if I can raise that many cents! What price?

GEORGE—How much could you afford to give? or, in other words, how much money have you?

KITTY—Seven cents; oh, what a beauty it is!

GEORGE—(*Very importantly*)—Our price, exactly, lacking a half cent; imported articles are very dear now; but let me see; considering, Kitty, that it is you, and your custom is worth something to us, we'll throw off a half cent. Shall I do it up for you, miss?

KITTY—Yes; here, (*counting out rusty pennies,*) one, two, three, four, five, six, seven; that's it.

GEORGE—She's worth every cent of it!

KITTY—Is she named?

GEORGE—(*Looking intently into a day-book*)—Yes, her name is Victoria Eugenia!

KITTY—But I don't like Victry Ugia! Would it hurt to change it?

GEORGE—Not a bit; call her anything you like: Susanna Maria, or Jane Elizabeth, or Matilda Ann.

KITTY—I'll call her Milly, wont that do?

GEORGE—First rate; nice and short. Yes, call her Milly.

KITTY—(*Kissing the doll*)—Oh, Milly, darling Milly, how I do love you. I'll make you a nice little bed when we get home, and we'll have such lots of fun; I wouldn't take seven times seven cents for you, my beauty, my precious beauty. [*Exit.*

Enter CELIA, *a very stylish-looking little lady.*

[GEORGE *bows very low, asking what she will have.*]

CELIA—A doll, a fine doll—would prefer one dressed as a bride—I believe that is the latest style—and it must be from Paris.

GEORGE—Our assortment, miss, is very fine; however, we have but one bride—here she is.

(*Holding up a beautiful doll.*)

CELIA—(*Fingering the dress*)—Is this real point lace?

GEORGE—Yes, that *is* point lace, no imitation about that.

CELIA—What price?

GEORGE—Ten dollars.

CELIA—Only ten, here it is; let me have her in a box!

GEORGE—(*Handing the box*)—We'll have some higher priced ones, with *real'er* point lace, when our ship comes in.

CELIA—No doubt. Good morning. [*Exit.*

[*Curtain.*]

SCENE II.—CAPTAIN HUTTON, seated, wiping his spectacles.

Enter CELIA, *pouting and half crying.*

CAPTAIN HUTTON—I'm sorry, my dear, that the doll doesn't suit you; but why didn't you go and buy it yourself? My little pet told me she got a perfect beauty at the toy shop—a perfect beauty.

CELIA—I did go, that's what makes me mad! I went and got the paltry thing, and gave ten dollars for it. No doubt, if I'd waited till the new lot came, and saved up ten more dollars, I could have suited myself. I don't know who that pet of yours is; but I suppose she spent a nice lot of money, and got the beauty of the establishment!

CAPTAIN HUTTON—Ha, ha, ha. (*Calls.*) Come here, Kitty; bring your doll, and show my niece—she is crying, because you have the prettiest one. Come, show it to us.

KITTY—(*With the doll wrapped in a shawl as she rocks it tenderly*)—Hush-a-by, hush-a-baby! Don't cry, little girl. I'll let you play with it; but don't, oh, don't ask me to part with her, my own Milly; and (*coaxingly*) don't be mad at me for having a pretty doll. I never had one of my *very* own before; and the minute I set eyes on this, I went about wild with joy.

CELIA—Let me see the doll.

KITTY—(*Half unwraps it, then pauses*)—You wont snatch it?

CELIA—Oh, girl, how you will have her dress crushed!

KITTY—(*Holds it up delightedly*)—Don't you wish she was yours?

[CELIA, *with a little affected scream, faints; and the uncle holds his sides with laughter.*]

[*Curtain.*]

THE CENSUS TAKER.

CHARACTERS:—MRS. SMITH.
SAMANTHY, addicted to poetry.
SAM, a ten-year old Boy.
MRS. HARRIS, the Neighbor.
CENSUS MARSHAL.

SCENE.—SAMANTHY, in a soiled wrapper, loose hair, and inky fingers, sits with portfolio in lap, trying to write.

Enter SAM, with cap on back of head, whistling, and bringing kite, knife, stick, and tacks.

SAM—Say, sis, where's ma?

SAMANTHY—Over to Mis' Harris's. (SAM *whittles on floor.*) You had better not let her catch you whittlin' on her clean floor!

SAM—You can clean it up.

SAMANTHY—Do I look like it?

SAM—I'm going to fix my kite, anyhow. Who's afraid of her?

Enter MRS. SMITH.

MRS. SMITH—Samuel! (SAM *drops knife and tacks, picks up, and sits down farther back.*) What be you a-doin'?

SAM—I was just a-makin' my kite.

MRS. SMITH—I'll "kite" you, if you don't stop whittlin'! (*Takes broom. A knock.*) Come!

Enter CENSUS MARSHAL.

CENSUS MARSHAL—Good morning!

MRS. SMITH—(*Grumblingly*)—Mornin'. Take a cheer? (*Dusting one with apron.*)

CENSUS MARSHAL—Thanks.

MRS. SMITH—Needn't mind about anything for *that*.

CENSUS MARSHAL—Madam, I'm commissioned by the United States Government to collect—

Mrs. Smith—Aint got nothin' to *give;* another feller 'round beggin' *last* week!

Census Marshal—You don't understand me, madam; I am simply authorized—

Mrs. Smith—I should *think* so!

Census Marshal—To take the Census!

[Mrs. Smith, *indignantly sweeping the dust into his face, he moves back, and places hat, with papers and gloves in it, on the table.* Sam *puts on hat and gloves, and takes papers for kite-tail.*]

Mrs. Smith—(*Very loud*)—You can't *take* none of my senses!

Census Marshal—You will please remember that one of *my* senses is peculiarly *acute;* and I can hear perfectly, if you don't speak half as loud!

Mrs. Smith—You'll have to be *"cuter"* than I think you be, if you *take* anything here!

Census Marshal—Are you the *head* of this family, madam?

Mrs. Smith—Well, yes; that's what folks say.

Census Marshal—I mean—have you a husband?

Mrs. Smith—O yes, when he's to hum; but he aint to hum to-day, 'cause I sent him down to Seth Browns's, to get a pound of candles. (*Sweeping.*)

Sam—Say, ma, old Brown says he wont trust you no more!

Mrs. Smith—Samuel!

Census Marshal—What is your husband's name?

Mrs. Smith—'Liphalet!

Census Marshal—Hasn't he any other?

Mrs. Smith—Yes, sir—Ebenezer! *his* mother and Ebenezer Jones kep' company for years, kinder; that is, he used to take her to spellin' schools, and huskin's, and sich; but when *he* went to sea, and wasn't heard from in six hull months, and my man's father kinder hung 'round, and being good-looking and fore-handed, she just up and married him, and named her first boy arter both on 'em— 'Liphalet Ebenezer.

CENSUS MARSHAL—My goodness!

SAM—And *my* name's John Samuel. Uncle John run off to Californy, after he stole that horse.

MRS. SMITH—'Taint no such thing! Sam, if you ever tell *where* he went to ag'in, I'll flog you; there!

CENSUS MARSHAL—Hope I haven't got to hear the whole family history. But what do the neighbors call him?

MRS. SMITH—Squire, mostly.

CENSUS MARSHAL—(*Aside*)—Doesn't she know anything? (*To* SAMANTHY.) Young lady, will you tell me the name of the man of this house?

SAMANTHY—Certainly. Smith; S-m-y-t-h-e!

CENSUS MARSHAL—(*Writing in his book, and reading aloud*)—"Eliphalet Ebenezer S-m-i-t-h."

SAMANTHY—Oh, that horrid man!

CENSUS MARSHAL—What's his occupation?

MRS. SMITH—His what?

CENSUS MARSHAL—What does he work at?

MRS. SMITH—Oh, as to that, he don't do much, my man don't; he's weak in the back, and work don't agree with him fust rate; and being of a sociable sort of mind, he sets 'round to the tavern mostly.

SAMANTHY—Oh, mother!

CENSUS MARSHAL—How much land have you?

MRS. SMITH—(*Leaning on her broom, and pointing out the window*)—Well, there's the three-corn'ed lot over east, (*pointing*,) where we had turnips last year, and that one jining onto Job Harris's forty-acre; but that's so stunny, that it haint never been plowed, and he took care of Job's melon-patch on shares—

Sam—When they got *ripe!*

Census Marshal—Keep to your own property!

Mrs. Smith—*That* aint much; just this 'ere house-lot; the rest is mortgaged.

Census Marshal—(*Writing and reading aloud*)—Let me see—acre, acre-and-a-half, two acres. Well! have you any horses?

Mrs. Smith—No! Eliphalet thinks them's too resky property.

Sam—Why, yes we have, ma!

Mrs. Smith—No we haint, nuther; what do you mean?

Sam—That old saw-horse, down in the shanty.

(*Goes to driving tacks with knife.*)

Mrs. Smith—(*Approvingly*)—Now, Samuel!

(Samanthy *giggles.*)

Census Marshal—Have you any other stock?

Mrs. Smith—Just one load of 'em, that Farmer Bailey give us to feed our cow.

Census Marshal—Then you have one cow?

(*Writing.*)

Mrs. Smith—Who denied it?

Sam—And she gives such *awful* rich milk; **ma** always has to water it, before selling Mis' Harris any.

Mrs. Smith—Samuel! you tell that ag'in, and I'll lick you within an inch of your life!

Census Marshal—I forgot to inquire about the children. Say them over, slowly, and I'll write them down.

Mrs. Smith—(*Counting on fingers very slowly*)—Well, there's 'Liphalet, named after his father, that's one; Samanthy, named after me, is two; Ne'amiah, but he's married, that's four; Peter, he's working for Bailey, so *we* aint got to pay for him; and Desire, she's the seventh, isn't she? Let me see! 'Liphalet, named after his father; Samanthy, named—

Census Marshal—*I* don't *desire* you should repeat them; go on!

Mrs. Smith—And Ne'amiah is four, and Samuel is five, and Sary Ann—but she's the baby, so we wont count *her* in either; Jim and Peggy's the twins, seven—and the other's at school.

Census Marshal—Others! How *many* others? Now their ages?

Mrs. Smith—Whose?

Census Marshal—Oh, 'Liphalet's, Ne'amiah's, etc.

Mrs. Smith—I wonder if I can tell! Ebenezer is— (Census Marshal *writes again.*) Well, now, I wouldn't a-thought he was *that* old; why, he was growin' on two when Jeff Smith—he's *his* cousin—married Sophy Jones —she's *my* cousin—and their oldest is big enough to come skylarkin' 'round here Sunday nights. *She (pointing to* Samanthy) is just his age, lacking six months. Next one's two year older than Peter; and he's—

(*Pointing to* Sam, *who snatches off hat, etc.*)

Census Marshal—How old *are* you, Bub?

Sam—A whole year littler than Bill Coon; but when he said as how I dasn't, I just told him I wasn't the man to take no sass, and I just at him, *I did*, and I'll lick him more, yet.

Samanthy—Where *does* he get that slang?

Mrs. Smith—(*To* Sam)—You aint to fight no more! (*To* Census Marshal.) Why, see here, reckon it yourself; he was born the May after the brindle cow killed herself with turnips—you see—

Census Marshal—No, I don't see, and I don't *want* to! Got any poultry?

Mrs. Smith—(*Aside*)—Tetchy, aint he? (*Aloud.*) Yes, Samanthy writ lots of it. (*To* Samanthy) Say, supposin' you tell him some of your pieces.

Samanthy—(*Affectedly*)—I only consult the muses as a recreation, sir, when the lambent fire burns so brightly in my brain; I have no other way of relieving my over-taxed mental faculties.

Sam—I say, sis, did you ever try cold water, to put out the fire?

Samanthy—Oh, that horrid boy!

Mrs. Smith—(*To* Sam)—Stop your noise, sir! (*To* Samanthy.) Just tell over the names of some of the prettiest ones. *Do!*

Samanthy—Well, there's "The Ode to the Moon," and "Thou modest Violet that opes thy Eye"—

Sam—"To every—body—passin' by!"

(Census Marshal *laughs*.)

Samanthy—(*To* Sam)—Shut up!

Census Marshal—I mean, hens, ducks, geese, and the like.

Mrs. Smith—Oh! Well, there's three white ones, one black pullet, one speckled, one that's blind, and one with her feet froze off. Counted 'em?

Sam—And two ruseters!

Census Marshal—Seven in all. (*Writes*.)

Enter Mrs. Harris, *with shawl over her head.*

Mrs. Harris—Mis' Smith, be you goin' to take care of that yearlin' of your'n, or not? My man, he says he'll shut him up in the pound! [*Exit*.

Mrs. Smith—Shut him up in the pond, will he? I suppose she means he'll drownd him! He'd better try it!

Sam—I tell you, he's a beauty, all red; the one *this* year is spotted.

Census Marshal—I'll put those in with the other stock. (*Writes. Rises.*) Well, madam, I believe that is all; I thank you for your information.

Mrs. Smith—I'm sure you're welcome to all the *inflammation* you've got out of me.

Census Marshal—(*Turns and snatches things, while he shakes and talks to* Sam)—You young rascal! (*Looks for papers in hat.*) What have you done with my papers?

Sam—(*Whining*)—I did n't think you'd care; so I took 'em for the tail of my kite.

Census Marshal—(*Leaves the room, muttering*)—I'd "kite" you, if I were your mother! [*Exit.*

Sam—Thank my stars, you never will be my mother.

Samanthy—Mother, will you chastise that boy, while I retire to revel in my accustomed flights of fancy?

Mrs. Smith—Do you mean *lick* him? That I will!

[*Curtain.*]

THE RETURNED BROTHER.

CHARACTERS:—Washington Watson, just returned.
John Watson, rich Brother.
Susan Kendall, Washington's Sister.

Scene.—A room in a hotel. Washington Watson discovered.

Washington—Home once more! Home from California! When I left this place, I was young and strong; now I am old and broken down; but I have money in abundance. I want to end my days here. I want to rest in peace. I have sent for my brother and sister; and, in these seedy garments, they will readily suppose that I have brought but little of the gold dust with me. Somebody's at the door, I think. (*Opens door.*)

Enter John Watson.

Washington—I suppose you are my brother John?

John—Yes. (*They shake hands.*) I came in answer to the request of your messenger.

Washington—I am glad to see you. How have you prospered?

John—Oh, I have been getting along miserably.

Washington—You wear good clothes. That's a sign of prosperity. Look at my clothes.

John—Yes, I have observed them. You did not prosper then, in California?

Washington—I lived comfortably. The climate is delightful. But I am an old man—several years older than you—and I have a desire to end my days here. You do not object to my taking up my abode with you?

John—Well—no—yes—that is. To tell the whole truth about the matter, Washington, my house is small, and I have a large family. It would not be pleasant for you there.

Washington—Oh, I can get along splendidly! I am fond of young folks.

John—Yes, but you know—

Washington—Oh, I understand. You think because I am old, I will make trouble in the household. But don't be alarmed. I am not quarrelsome. (*Knock at the door.*) My sister, I suppose. (*Opens the door.*)

Enter Mrs. Susan Kendall.

Mrs. Kendall—(*Throwing her arms around* Washington)—Oh, Washington, you have returned at last! I am delighted to see you. But why didn't you come to our house? Why did you stop here?

Washington—I thought it would be right and proper for me to stop here, until I had found out whether I would be welcome or not.

Mrs. Kendall—Washington! Why do you talk so? Did you for a moment suppose that we would not be glad to see you?

Washington—Well, I didn't know. This is a queer world, and those we consider very dear friends are sometimes bitter enemies.

Mrs. Kendall—I am surprised that you should for an instant suppose that we would not be very glad to see you.

Washington—But you see I am poorly dressed. Would you care to keep me awhile at your house?

Mrs. Kendall—Certainly, we will keep you! Are you not my brother? We are not wealthy. We have a large family, and my husband is a cripple; but do you, for a moment, suppose that I would not be glad to have you stay with us, as long as you please?

Washington—But here's my wealthy brother, John, who doesn't feel inclined to take me, and why should I thrust myself upon you? He is rich, they say, and you are poor.

John—Well, you see—Susan, you understand how it is. We have a large family, and our house is small, and a stranger coming in, is apt to cause trouble.

Mrs. Kendall—But, John, Washington is our brother.

John—I know, and he had as much money to start with as I had. If he wandered over the world, and spent it all, it is no fault of mine.

Mrs. Kendall—John, I am astonished!

John—Are you, indeed?

Mrs. Kendall—You are becoming too grasping and avaricious. You can not take your money with you when you go down to the grave.

John—Susan, it isn't necessary for you to commence to preach to me. I think I can attend to my own affairs.

Washington—Yes, go forward and lay up money—you may need it all.

John—And if you and Susan had been more economical, you would have been in better circumstances to-day. But I can't stand here talking all day; I have business to attend to. (*Going.*)

WASHINGTON—You are not going to see me thrown out upon the cold charities of the world—you are not going to allow me to go to the poor-house, are you?

JOHN—Susan says she will keep you. She seems to be seeking trouble, and if she desires to make you a member of her household, you shouldn't growl. "Beggars shouldn't be choosers," you know.

WASHINGTON—And you will not reach out your hand to save me from the poor-house?

JOHN—(*Testily*)—I don't see any use in making so much fuss about it. Didn't you get as much money as I? If you made a bad use of it—if you squandered it—you can not blame me. You should have taken care of your money. If you had done so, you would not have been going around now trying to sponge off your relations.

WASHINGTON—Stop. I have heard enough. How much money do you suppose I have?

JOHN—(*Sneeringly*)—Well, from your appearance, I should say you have twenty-five cents.

WASHINGTON—Shrewd guesser! Well, sir, I wish to tell you that I have money sufficient to buy out half a dozen such small men as you. I have at least five hundred thousand dollars, and I am happy to say that neither you nor any of your family shall lay your hands on a penny of it. My money was not made to be handled by small-souled people. I wished to find out how my brother and sister would treat me. I am satisfied. I will make my home with my sister. She shall want for nothing, and at my death my money shall belong to her and her children. Good morning, most noble brother. I have had my say, and you can retire.

John—But, Washington, you do not consider. I explained to you that I had a small house, and a large family. Of course I would like to have you stay with me.

Washington—Susan, come. If he will not retire we will. (*To* John.) Your house has suddenly become larger, but the five hundred thousand dollars didn't make it become so! Oh, no, of course not! Come, Susan, I do not wish to hold any further conversation with him.

[*Exit* Washington *and* Susan.

John—Well, now, haven't I put my foot in it? Who would have supposed that a man dressed in that style was the possessor of five hundred thousand dollars? Just my luck! I declare I feel angry enough to howl.

[*Exit* John.

[*Curtain.*]

AFTER A FASHION.

CHARACTERS:—Mrs. Nelson.
Mrs. Armstrong, a Caller.
Minnie, Mrs. Armstrong's Daughter.

Scene.—A parlor.

Enter Mrs. Nelson, *with a book in her hand.*

Mrs. Nelson—(*Solus*)—There! I've got my morning work all done. I'll just get a lunch at noon for myself, and then I'll have nothing to do until John comes home to-night. There's some mending that ought to be done, and those shirts of John's must be made before long, for he is complaining about his old ones. But I don't know that I'm going to be tied up sewing all the time. I believe I'll hire those shirts made, and set the cost of their making down as household expenses. John will never find it out. I'm going to have one day to myself anyhow, to take solid comfort in. Here's this novel that I haven't been able to look at since yesterday forenoon, and I left off right in the most interesting part. And I'm so afraid John will find out I am reading it before I have finished it. Now I will sit down and enjoy myself. (*Seats herself in a chair and opens the book.*) Hark! Didn't I hear a carriage stop before the house? (*Gets up and looks out.*) I did. And if that odious Mrs. Armstrong isn't getting out of it! She's got that disgusting child of hers with her, and I know she's come to spend the day. Oh, dear! Was there ever anything more vexatious? Mrs. Armstrong herself is bad enough, but that stupid child is worse. I often think I am just like an old hen. I like my own chickens well enough, but I feel like cracking every other hen's chicks on the head.

[MRS. ARMSTRONG *knocks*. MRS. NELSON *lays her book on the table and opens the door.*]

Enter MRS. ARMSTRONG *and* MINNIE.

MRS. NELSON—My dear Mrs. Armstrong! (*Kisses her.*) How glad I am to see you! And how kind of you to come! Now sit right down and let me take your bonnet and cloak.

[*Offers her a chair.* MRS. ARMSTRONG *and* MINNIE *sit down.*]

MRS. ARMSTRONG—Oh, no, no, I can not stay long.

MRS. NELSON—(*Aside*)—Oh, I'm so glad! (*To* MRS. ARMSTRONG.) Not stay long? Why, you have come to spend the day with me, of course. I was so lonesome this morning that I did not know what to do with myself, and as soon as I saw you drive up, I said, now there is that dear delightful woman, who always knows when to do a kind action, come to keep me company to-day, and what a pleasant time we shall have. Now *wont* you, *can't* you make up your mind to stay?

Mrs. Armstrong—I wish I could, you dear woman, but it is impossible.

Mrs. Nelson—You don't know how disappointed I am! (*Aside.*) It is such a relief to know I wont have to get dinner, and nothing in the house but a little cold meat. (*To* Mrs. Armstrong.) Well, since you *wont* stay let us make the best of the little time we have. And how are you, dear?

Mrs. Armstrong—I'm quite well, I thank you. And how have you been since I saw you last?

Mrs. Nelson—Tolerably well. Only I am so lonesome. You know John leaves me at home all day, and the children go to school, and you never come to see me. And how is this little darling? (*Kisses* Minnie.)

Minnie—Very well.

Mrs. Armstrong—Minnie, why don't you ask the lady how she is?

Minnie—Because I don't want to know.

Mrs. Armstrong—Oh, Minnie! (*To* Mrs. Nelson.) Well, you know children will be children.

Mrs. Nelson—The dear child! It is such a blessing to have children candid and truthful. If grown folks were only so, how much better the world would be. I always try to set my children an example. (*Aside.*) The little unmannerly cub! I would soon teach her better if she was my child!

Mrs. Armstrong—Yes, Minnie is very truthful, and I am glad she is so. But how do you spend these long days?

Mrs. Nelson—Oh, how can you ask me that, and yourself the mistress of a family? You must know a mother and housekeeper always finds plenty to do. There are always mending and making on hand, enough to more than fill up one's leisure moments. Just as I heard your carriage drive to the door, I was about to get out the muslin to make my husband some shirts. I never have one moment of time to rest or to improve my mind.

Mrs. Armstrong—You poor woman! You must not overwork yourself.

Mrs. Nelson—How can I help it? You know it is the lot of all women. If we can only make our husbands happy, and bring up our children to be useful members of society, we should never be discontented or complain.

Mrs. Armstrong—(*Takes up book from table*)—What is this? Oh, I see, I hope you have not been reading it.

Mrs. Nelson—That book? Oh, no! I wouldn't look at it for anything. My husband brought it home last night for me to read, but I told him I hadn't a moment of time to do so.

Mrs. Armstrong—My husband said it wasn't a proper book at all for a woman to read, or even for a man.

Mrs. Nelson—Is it possible? I didn't suspect it, for I haven't looked into it. I wonder John brought it to me. But then he knows *I* can safely read anything, for my principles are so firmly fixed. How happy a woman should be when her husband can trust her! Well, I'm glad you told me, for if I had found a little time after my sewing was done, I might have turned over a few pages. And though my husband is so careless, *I* think women can not be too particular what they read.

Mrs. Armstrong—Yes, so I think. But really, I must be going.

Mrs. Nelson—Don't think of it. You haven't stayed any time yet.

Mrs. Armstrong—(*Rising*)—But I must, indeed I wish I *could* stay longer.

Mrs. Nelson—Well, if you *must* go, I can't compel you to stay. But *do* come soon and spend the entire day with me. You know there is nobody whom I am so glad to see as yourself. And you must be sure to bring this little darling with you.

Mrs. Armstrong—Well, do come and see me, my dear Mrs. Nelson.

Mrs. Nelson—I will certainly, if I can ever spare the time from my work. (*They kiss.*)

Mrs. Armstrong—Good morning.

Mrs. Nelson—Good morning, dear. (*Exit* Mrs. Armstrong *and* Minnie.) There, she's gone at last, and I'm *so* glad. The mean, spying thing! She thought she had caught me on that novel, but I don't think she found out much. If she waits until I want to see her before she comes again, she will be old and gray. My whole morning has been wasted with her call. So now I will go and take my lunch, and then make another attempt to sit down and finish the book before John comes home and discovers me reading it.

[*Exit* Mrs. Nelson

[*Curtain.*]

A FRIGHTENED LODGER.

CHARACTERS:—HEZEKIAH SCRUGGINS.
ALEXANDER ADDISON.
PAT MULRAVEY.
LANDLORD.

SCENE.—Room in a Hotel.

Enter HEZEKIAH.

HEZ.—Wall, I 'spose I'll hev tew stop here and stay over night. This ain't much of a room, neither, tew put sich a feller as Hezekiah Scruggins intew. The landlord sez as heow they are awfully crowded, and if another feller should happen tew come, I s'pose he'd chuck him in along o' me. Neow I'd rayther not hev a companyun on the present occasion, but I reckon ef anybody comes in it will hev tew be endoored. I 'most wish I hadn't come tew this big agercultural fair. It ain't nothin' but push and scrouge from mornin' till night. (*Sits down.*) I'm most tarnation tired. I've been a trampin' reound all this blessed day, and haven't seen nothin' of much acccount neither. I wish I was tew hum. If I know myself I'll strike eout fur that same hum to-morrow evenin'. (*Noise outside.*) Hullo! thar's a trampin' at the door. I 'spose my pardner is a comin'. If I am tew have a companyun, I hope he'll be a respectable-lookin' feller. (*Door is opened, and* LANDLORD *ushers in* ALEXANDER ADDISON. HEZEKIAH *rises. Exit* LANDLORD.)

ALEX.—Well, my friend, it seems that we are to lodge together to-night.

HEZ.—Yaas, so it seems. This ain't an awful good

room, but I reckon we'll hev tew put up with it, seein as heow all the houses are so much crowded.

Alex.—I feel very tired, and shall sit down to rest. Be seated, my friend; don't let my coming disturb you.

Hez.—No, yeou ain't disturbin' me, not in the least (*Aside.*) That feller's got a quare look abeout him. I'm mighty 'fraid thar's somethin' wrong.

Alex.—Why don't you sit down and make yourself comfortable? If you have travelled around as much as I have to-day you certainly feel like resting.

Hez.—I guess I'll step reound a spell; I don't feel like sittin'. (*Aside.*) By thunder, I believe that's the crazy man that is a runnin' areound. He answers tew the description.

Alex.—(*Goes to door and locks it*)—I guess I'll shut out all intruders. That money-loving landlord would likely crowd a couple more into this room if they should ask for lodging. Well, we are bosses now, Mr. —— I forgot to ask your name.

Hez.—My name is Hezekiah Scruggins, at yeour sarvice.

Alex.—And mine is Alexander Addison.

Hez.—(*Aside*)—Good gracious! I don't know what on airth I'll dew. But I must git eout o' this. It'll never dew tew stay here. He has locked the door, and one of his crazy spells will come on soon. By gosh, I don't know what's tew be done. I am in the third story, and can't jump eout of a window—no sir! that might make a finish of me. But I must do somethin' soon. What an ugly eye he has!

Alex.—(*Aside*)—That's a rascally-looking fellow. He doesn't seem inclined to talk, and he goes around as if he wanted to do something desperate. I really think he is a robber or a pickpocket. They say there were plenty of them on the fair-grounds to-day. I wish I was out of this.

Hez.—(*Aside*)—I guess as heow I'll holler. I'm most afeared tew dew so, tew, fur he would immediately spring upon me. (*To* Alex.) Yeou'd better unlock that door agin, hadn't yeou?

Alex.—And why should I unlock the door?

Hez.—(*In a frightened tone*)—I—I—guess I'll—go deown stairs agin.

Alex.—All right, you can go. Will you come back? (*As* Alexander *goes to unlock the door he passes close to* Hezekiah, *who thinks he is trying to catch hold of him.* Hez. *jumps to one side and shouts:*)

Hez.—Murder! murder!

Alex.—(*Aside*)—That's a pickpocket; I feel certain of it. He is trying to get up an excitement for the purpose of robbing somebody. (*Advancing towards* Hez.) I know your true character, sir, and I have a good mind to knock you down.

Hez.—It's coming on! It's coming on! Oh, what will I dew? Good gracious! what'll I dew?

Alex.—None of your nonsense, now; I understand you, and if you raise any more noise I'll give you a beating.

Hez.—(*Shouting*)—Oh, gracious! let me eout! Landlord! Landlord!

Alex.—Stop your noise, I say. You are a pickpocket; I know you are, and I'll have you arrested if you don't clear out.

Hez.—Oh, he's gittin' wusser and wusser! I wish I had stayed to hum. (*Knock at door. Opened by* Alex. *Enter* Landlord *and others.*)

Landlord—What's the meaning of this rumpus?

Hez.—Yeou've put a crazy man in here with me.

It is awful. I'm scared tew death. He has tried to ketch me. Oh, it is dreadful!

ALEX.—There's not a word of truth in that, and he knows it. I am aware of his true character. He is one of the many pickpockets that were on the fairgrounds to-day. Look out for your pockets! He is only trying to get up an excitement to get a crowd gathered around.

HEZ.—That's allers the way crazy people talk. I read abeout him in the papers, and I've hearn people talk abeout him, and he answers tew the description exactly. I tell yeou, yeou'd better look eout. He may do a great deal of mischief.

ALEX.—(*To* LANDLORD)—Don't mind him, he is frightened about nothing. I doubt not you have heard of me. My name is Alexander Addison, and I flatter myself that I do not act very much like a madman.

LANDLORD—(*To* HEZ.)—My friend, I think you have become frightened unnecessarily. And (*To* ALEX.) I think you wrong the gentleman when you accuse him of being a pickpocket. My advice is, make friends again, and sit down and rest yourselves.

ALEX.—No, sir; I do not choose to room with a man who has insulted me by saying that I look like a crazy person. I'll sleep in the street first.

HEZ.—Wall, I don't keer where yeou sleep, but I'm mighty sartin yeou'll not sleep with me. Yeou may be all right abeout the upper story, but I doubt it the blamedest.

ALEX.—Be careful, greeny, or I'll knock you down.

HEZ.—There! I told yeou he warn't square; the fit's comin' on agin. Better git him away as quick as possible.

Alex.—Dunce! I will go. I don't wish to be in the same house with such a scarey youth.

Landlord—Stay, I think I can accommodate you. And (*To* Pat Mulravey, *who came in with the* Landlord) stranger, as you wanted lodging, I think I can accommodate you, too. (*To* Hez.) This gentleman came in a few minutes ago. I will let him room with you to-night, and I hope you will get along smoothly.

Hez.—(*Aside*)—He's a rough-looking customer. (*To* Landlord.) I'll try and endoor him.

Pat—What's that ye say, ye blackguard? Endoor me! Be the howly St. Patrick, I giss I'll have to do all the endoorin. Ye'r a mighty outspoken chap, onyhow, and I've a mind to give ye a tap on the nose jist to bring ye to yer sinsis.

Hez.—I beg yeour parding, sir; it was a mere slip of the tongue.

Pat—Well, be mighty careful not to let yer tongue slip again or be the powers I'll give it a twist that will sthop it av slippin'.

Landlord—It seems that you can get along together, and so I will leave you.

Pat—Niver fear about that, Mr. Landlord; we'll git along first rate. This is a nice enough feller, on'y a little scarey about crazy people.

[*Exit* Landlord, Alexander, *and others.*

Pat—(*Aside*)—Be the powers, I'll give him a scare worth talkin about. I'll act the crazy man a dale of a sight better'n that other feller did, and if I don't scare him right, thin my name isn't Pat Mulravey. (*To* Hez.) Me name is Pat Mulravey. And what is your name?

Hez.—Hezekiah Scruggins, at yeour sarvice, sir.

Pat—Hezekiah Scruggins, at ye'r sarvice, sir! Well,

that's a mighty long name. I'll call ye Scrooggins for short. Yez thought that was a crazy feller, didn't yez?

Hez.—Yaas, I had hearn tell that thar was a crazy man loose, and I had read abeout him, and as the feller answered tew the description I thought he must be the one.

Pat—Faix, I am the crazy feller—I im that, mesilf I am as crazy as iver Nickey Mulrooney was. Nickey Mulrooney lived in the town av Cork and was a broth av a boy.

Hez.—Pooh! Yeou air tryin tew frighten me. I rayther guess I'll not be so much alarmed ag'in.

Pat—(*Aside*)—I'll fetch him yet, see if I don't. (*To* Hez.) I'm a rale pacible b'y until the spill comes upon me and thin I git mighty obstepeevious.

Hez.—Obstepeevious! what is that?

Pat—I'll tell ye, sir. Whin a b'y gits obstepeevious he can do most onything; he can fight, run, jump, knock fellers down and tear round like the very old Nick. I am an Irishman, sir.

Hez.—I supposed yeou were. The Irish air a clever people.

Pat—Faix, and ye'r right there, and they're a mighty smashin set too whin they get into the smashin humor. That crazy Nickey Mulrooney I was tellin yez of, he could fling four or five b'ys out av a third story windy before breakfast in the marnin, and make nothin av it, sir. And I tell ye he made things sthand around whin he got into a bit av a shindy. Be the powers, I feel mesilf gittin a little obstepeevious whin I think about it, and I've a kind of a notion jist to thry and show ye how he made things jingle whin the sphell was on him.

Hez.—Oh, Mr. Mulravey, yeou needn't dew that! I'll take yeour word for it. (*Aside.*) Good gracious! I believe he *is* a crazy man. But I don't like to run away. Jemimy Wiggins allers said I was a skeery feller, but I'll try and be brave on this occasion; I'll stand and face the danger.

Pat—Be the powers, that snakin landlord shan't git in here any more. He's an ugly blackguard, onyhow, and I'll kape him from sthickin his nose into this place.

Hez.—Oh, dear! he has locked the door. I wonder if he isn't only tryin tew frighten me. But he looks desp'rit. (*To* Pat.) Why did yeou lock the door, Mr. Mulravey?

Pat—That oogly landlord shan't coom a walkin in here jist whiniver we git up a little breeze. I'll larn him better than to do that. Faix, and I will. You and me may have a bit av a shindy soon and it'll be betther to kape that blackguard av a landlord on the outside. Don't ye think so, Mr. Scrooggins?

Hez.—Wall, neow, tew tell yeou the truth abeout the matter, Mr. Mulravey, I'd prefer to have the door unlocked.

Pat—And I'd prefer to have it locked, and shure that's jist where we differ, Misther Scrooggins. I feel about as sthrong as a forty horse ingine and I giss I'll be boss on this occasion. (Pat *gets up on a chair and crows like a rooster.*) Whoop! This is better than Donnybrook fair. This is the bist fair I've been at in the whole blissid counthry. (*Shouts.*) Hurra! I want to knock somebody down. Hurra for a bit av a shindy!

Hez.—(*Aside*)—Oh. gracious! he must be crazy! I wish Mr. Addison had stayed here.

Pat—Come here, me darlint. Let us have a bit av a jig. Ain't yez a thripper?

Hez.—No, no; keep off! I don't want yeou tew touch me. Go and dance by yeourself.

Pat—Faix, an' I can't do that. It's agin the natur of the Mulraveys to dance alone whin there's a foine-lookin famale about. Come, Miss Scrooggins, let us have a dance.

Hez.—Oh, no, no! Keep off or I'll shout.

Pat—Shout! An what good will shoutin do, I'd like to know. Faix, the landlord is down in the first sthory and ye might yill for an hour and he wouldn't hear anything at all, at all.

Hez.—I'll burst the door open if yeou don't stop bothering me.

Pat—Burst the door open! Ye blackguard, ye can't do that while I've got an arrum on me neck and a head on me showlder. Shure I could knock ye into the middle of Janewary afore ye'd know what I was about.

Hez.—(*Aside*)—Oh, if I was eout of this scrape I'd start for hum on the double quick. (*To* Pat.) Can't yeou sit deown for a while? I am tired and I think yeou ought tew be too.

Pat—Be two! Be me sowl, it's as much as I can do to be one. But if ye bees tired, Mr. Scrooggins, sit down and I'll sit on top av yez. There is only one substantial chair an' I wouldn't be mindin me manners if I'd sit on it and let ye squat on the flure by yersilf. (*In a loud voice.*) Sit down, Mr. Scrooggins, sit down. D'ye mind me now? Bedad if yez don't sit down I'll sthrike ye a lick abowt the middle and knock ye clane out av the windy.

Hez.—(*Sits on floor*)—Wall, I'll sit deown to accommodate yeou. I hope yeou'll be quiet neow.

Pat—(*Aside*)—Faix, I've got him purty badly scared.

I giss I'd betther boost him up a little and give nim a run around the ring. (*To* HEZ.) Mr. Scrooggins, git up. Yez has got to act "Black Hawk" and I'll be "Mazeppa" and we'll tear round the track jist as the horses did to-day at the fair. Won't that be fun?

HEZ.—(*Aside*)—Oh, how crazy he is! But he doesn't seem disposed tew dew anything desp'rit, and so I had better humor him. (*Gets up.*)

PAT—Now, thin, Mr. Scrooggins, yez may run once around the track, thin I'll set in and go it like lightnin. I giss it would be betther, Mr. Scrooggins, for ye to purtind to be ridin the Black Hawk horse, and I'll be ridin Mazeppa, and thin we can holler at thim and lick thim up and make thim sthreak it. Won't that be betther, Mr. Scrooggins?

HEZ.—Yes, anything to please yeou, Mr. Mulravey. But hadn't yeou better unlock the door before yeou commence?

PAT—Unlock the door, ye spalpeen? No, sir; don't ye know the horses might run out av the ring if the door was open? Bedad an I don't want the horses to git away. Now, Mr. Scrooggins, ye are to ride Black Hawk. Git on and make him go his bist, and I'll be afther ye in a twinklin. I'll give yez the word. *Go!* (HEZEKIAH *commences to run around the room.* PAT *stands in the centre and shouts.*) He'p! Hi! Git! Faster, ye lazy ould blackguard! Go it, now! Bedad, ye can't trot worth a cint. (HEZEKIAH *after running a few times round the room stops almost out of breath.*)

HEZ.—I thought yeou was a goin tew ride a hoss tew.

PAT—An so I am, me darlint. But I want to git ould Black Hawk perty well run down afore I set in. Now go it again. (PAT *shouts.* HEZEKIAH *commences to run again.*) Git up, Black Hawk, ye lazy ould black-guard! H'ep! Hi! Git along! Go it! Limber out, ye stiff ould spalpeen! Mr. Scrooggins, ye must holler at yer horse and purtind to be a lickin him. (HEZEKIAH *shouts and motions as if whipping his horse.*)

HEZ.—Hi! Git eout! Wake up, Black Hawk! G'lang!

PAT—Now, old Mazeppa, we'll go in. (*Follows after* HEZEKIAH, *shouting*) Hi! Go it, ye blackguard! He'p! Hi! Git along! Be jabers this is the biggest kind o' fun! Hi! Go it, Scrooggins! I'm gainin on yez! Hi! Git along, Scrooggins! (*Noise at door.*)

LANDLORD—(*Speaks outside*)—What is the meaning of all this noise? Open the door.

PAT—Don't mind him, Scrooggins. (*They continue running.*) Hi! Git along there, ye blackguard! Hi! Ho! Ye'r comin in on the home-stretch now. Hi!

LANDLORD—(*Shouting*)—Open the door, I say; open it instantly!

PAT—Scrooggins, go it! Ye'r ould Black Hawk is givin out. Go it! Hi! Be the powers I'm going to win the race. Hi!

LANDLORD—(*Shouts again*)—Open the door, I say, or I'll have you arrested. (*They stop running.*)

PAT—Scrooggins, darlint, the people bees comin to see the race. We'll let them in an thin we'll go it again. (*Goes to open the door.*)

HEZ.—(*Comes to front of stage*)—Oh, gracious! Oh, dear! I'm clean run deown. (*Panting.*) I'm all eout of breath. Oh, dear! (PAT *opens door. Enter* LANDLORD.)

LANDLORD—What is the meaning of all this noise? You have alarmed the whole house.

PAT—Faix, we've been havin a jolly time; it wint ahead av Donnybrook fair. Me and Scrooggins has been ridin around the ring. He rid Black Hawk and I rid Mazeppa. Oh, how we did make thim horses spin. We were jist comin in on the home-stretch. I tell yez, that Mazeppa is a darlint!

LANDLORD—Well, sir, I don't choose to have my room changed into a race-course. One of you must leave.

HEZ.—(*Still panting*)—I'll go! I'll go! I wouldn't stay here over night for a thousand dollars—by hokey, I wouldn't!

PAT—(*Aside*)—Be jabers, ould Black Hawk's about give out. (*To* HEZ.) Me darlint, I'd like ye'd sthay. Ye are a spinner to run, and I'd like to see ye go it again.

HEZ.—No! no! I'll not stay! I'd as leave stay in a lunatic asylum. (*To* LANDLORD.) Better look eout for him; he's a rail crazytick.

[*Exit* HEZEKIAH.

PAT—(*To* LANDLORD)—Be jabers, that's a badly scared b'y. He thought that other man was a madman, and I took a notion I'd be afther showin him what a rale madman was.

LANDLORD—Yes, and you have aroused all my lodgers. But I'll forgive you if you go to bed and keep quiet the rest of the night.

PAT—Faix, and I'll do that, fur I'm mighty tired 'fter batin old Sweepstakes.

[*Exit* LANDLORD.

[*Curtain.*]

Choice Humor
By Charles C. Shoemaker
For Reading and Recitation

To prepare a book of humor that shall be free from anything that is coarse or vulgar on the one hand, and avoid what is flat and insipid on the other, is the difficult task which the compiler set for himself, and which he has successfully accomplished. The book has been prepared with the utmost care, and it will be found as interesting and attractive for private reading as it is valuable for public entertainment.

Choice Dialect
By Charles C. Shoemaker
For Reading and Recitation

This book will be found to contain a rare and valuable collection of Irish, German, Scotch, French, Negro, and other dialects, and to represent every phase of sentiment from the keenest humor or the tenderest pathos to that which is strongly dramatic. It affords to the amateur reader and the professional elocutionist the largest scope for his varied abilities, and is entirely free from anything that would offend the most refined taste.

Choice Dialogues
By Mrs. J. W. Shoemaker
For School and Social Entertainment

Entirely new and original. The topics have been arranged on a comprehensive plan, with reference to securing the greatest possible variety, and the matter has been specially prepared by a corps of able writers, their aim being to secure loftiness of conception, purity of tone, and adaptability to the needs of amateurs. It is an all-round dialogue book, being suited to children and adults, and to Sunday-schools and day-schools. It is conceded to be one of the best dialogue books in print.

THE PENN PUBLISHING COMPANY
925-27 FILBERT STREET PHILADELPHIA

Entertainment Books for Young People

Comic Dialogues
By John R. Dennis

This is the something "real funny," which every boy and girl prefers, but there is nothing coarse in it. It is suitable for school or church use anywhere. The dialogues are arranged for from two to a dozen or more children. A few, like "Vilikens" and "The Headless Horseman," employ music. "Our Lysander" is a real little play. Some of the dialogues are: Innocents Abroad, Artist's Dream, Aunt Dinah and Columbus, Taking the Census, Strictly Confidential, etc.

Humorous Dialogues *and* Dramas
By Charles C. Shoemaker

If there is anything more enjoyable than a humorous reading or recitation it is a keen, pointed, humorous dialogue. The compiler, with the largest resources and widest experience in literature for entertainment purposes, has produced one of the rarest, brightest, jolliest books of mirth-provoking dialogues ever published. Much of the matter was prepared especially for this work. The dialogues are adapted to old and young of both sexes, and while often keenly witty, are wholly free from coarseness and vulgarity.

Classic Dialogues *and* Dramas
By Mrs. J. W. Shoemaker

This unique work will prove not only interesting and profitable for purposes of public and social entertainment, but also instructive and valuable for private reading and study. The book comprises popular scenes judiciously selected from the plays of Shakespeare, Sheridan, Bulwer, Schiller, and other dramatists, and each dialogue is so arranged as to be complete in itself. Many of the exercises may be given as readings or recitals, and will prove acceptable to audiences of the highest culture and refinement.

THE PENN PUBLISHING COMPANY
925-27 FILBERT STREET PHILADELPHIA

Entertainment Books for Young People

Sterling Dialogues
By William M. Clark

The dialogues comprising this volume have been chosen from a large store of material. The contributions are from the pens of the most gifted writers in this field of literature, and the topics are so varied and comprehensive that they are readily adapted to the needs of Schools, Academies, and Literary Societies. They are especially suited for Social Gatherings and Home Amusement, as the staging required is simple and easily obtained.

Model Dialogues
By William M. Clark

The dialogues comprising this collection have been contributed by over thirty of America's best writers in this field of literature. They represent every variety of sentiment and emotion, from the extremely humorous to the pathetic. Every dialogue is full of life and action; the subjects are well chosen, and are so varied as to suit all grades of performers. The book is especially adapted for School Exhibitions, Literary Societies, and Sunday-school and Social Gatherings.

Standard Dialogues
By Rev. Alexander Clark, A. M.

The author's name is a guaranty of the excellence of this book. His long experience as a lecturer before Teachers' Institutes, and his close study of the teachers' needs, his lofty ideals of education and of life, his refinement of taste, diversity of attainment, and versatility of expression, all combine to qualify him in an eminent degree for the preparation of such a volume. For both teacher and entertainer this book has special points of merit, as the dialogues are interesting as well as instructive.

THE PENN PUBLISHING COMPANY
925-27 FILBERT STREET PHILADELPHIA

Entertainment Books for Young People

Schoolday Dialogues
By Rev. Alexander Clark, A. M.

This book of dialogues, prepared for use in School Entertainments, furnishes great diversity of sentiment and diction. Although for the most part composed of serious or pathetic subject-matter, there will be found many humorous dialogues and much good material for the little folks, as well as for the older ones. The staging and costuming are of the simplest character, and are so fully described as to make the task of preparation quite easy, even for the novice.

Popular Dialogues
By Phineas Garrett

The author's large experience in the Entertainment and Amusement field has qualified him for the preparation of a book of unusual merit. No work of this kind more fully meets the popular demand for interesting and refined entertainment. In this collection will be found dialogues to suit every occasion, either for public entertainment or for a social evening at home. Humor and pathos are pleasantly blended, and provision is made for the wants of the young and the old, the grave and the gay, the experienced and the inexperienced.

Excelsior Dialogues
By Phineas Garrett

This book is composed of original dialogues and colloquies designed for students in Schools and Academies, and prepared expressly for this work by a corps of professional teachers and writers. Comedy and tragedy are provided in due proportion, and the moral tone of the work is of the highest order. Teachers will here find just the material for which they have been searching, something with plot enough to hold the attention and that will command the best efforts of the older pupils.

THE PENN PUBLISHING COMPANY
925-27 FILBERT STREET PHILADELPHIA

Entertainment Books for Young People

Fancy Drills and Marches
By Alice M. Kellogg

Children enjoy drills, and this is the most successful drill book ever published. It has more than fifty new ideas—drills, marches, motion songs and action pieces. Among them are a Sifter Drill, Ribbon March with Grouping and Posing, Pink Rose Drill, Christmas Tree Drill, Delsarte Children, Zouave Drill, Wreath Drill and March, Glove Drill, Tambourine Drill, March of the Red, White and Blue. Teachers will be especially pleased with the care given to the exercises for the smaller children. All of the drills are fully illustrated.

Ideal Drills
By Marguerite W. Morton

This book contains a collection of entirely new and original drills, into which are introduced many unique and effective features. The fullest descriptions are given for the successful production of the drills, and to this end nearly 100 diagrams have been inserted showing the different movements. Everything is made so clear that anyone can use the drills without the slightest difficulty. Among the more popular and pleasing drills are: The Brownie, Taper, Maypole, Rainbow, Dumb-bell, Butterfly, Sword, Flower, Ring, Scarf, Flag, and Swing Song and Drill.

Eureka Entertainments

The title of this volume expresses in a nutshell the character of its contents. The weary searcher after material for any kind of entertainment will, upon examination of this book, at once exclaim, "I have found it." Here is just what is wanted for use in day-school, Sunday-school, at church socials, teas, and other festivals, for parlor or fireside amusement, in fact, for all kinds of school or home, public or private entertainments. The work is characterized by freshness and originality throughout.

THE PENN PUBLISHING COMPANY
925-27 FILBERT STREET PHILADELPHIA

Entertainment Books for Young People

Special Day Exercises
By Amos M. Kellogg

Almost every week in the school year has its birthday of a national hero or a great writer. Washington, Michael Angelo, Shakespeare, Longfellow, Holmes, Browning and Emerson are among those the children learn to know from this book. The holidays, Easter, Christmas, Thanksgiving, Memorial Day are not forgotten; and in between are many happy suggestions for tree planting, for bird and flower lessons, and debates.

Christmas Selections
By Rosamond Livingstone McNaught
For Readings and Recitations

Sunday schools, day schools, the home circle, all demand material for Christmas entertainments, and all want something new and appropriate. This book contains just what is wanted. Every piece is absolutely new, not a single one having previously been published in any book. It contains recitations, in prose and poetry, for every conceivable kind of public or private entertainment at Christmas time.

Holiday Selections
By Sara Sigourney Rice
For Readings and Recitations

The selections in this volume are adapted to all the different holidays of the year and are classified accordingly. Fully half of the pieces are for Christmas, but ample provision is also made for New Year's, St. Valentine's Day, Washington's Birthday, Easter, Arbor Day, Decoration Day, Fourth of July, and Thanksgiving. The pieces are unusually bright, and the variety under each holiday will afford the fullest opportunity for a satisfactory choice; the older students and the little ones alike will find something suited to their different degrees of ability.

THE PENN PUBLISHING COMPANY
925-27 FILBERT STREET PHILADELPHIA

Entertainment Books for Young People

Holiday Entertainments
By Charles C. Shoemaker

Absolutely new and original. There are few things more popular during the holiday season than Entertainments and Exhibitions, and there is scarcely anything more difficult to procure than new and meritorious material appropriate for such occasions. This book is made up of short dramas, dialogues, tableaux, recitations, etc., introducing many novel features that give the spice and sparkle so desirable for such occasions. It is adapted to the full round of holidays, containing features especially prepared for Christmas, New Year's, Washington's Birthday, Easter, Decoration Day, Fourth of July, and Thanksgiving.

Spring and Summer School Celebrations
By Alice M. Kellogg

This book shows how to capture "all outdoors" for the school room. Every warm weather holiday, including May Day, Memorial Day, Closing Day, is represented; for each the book offers from ten to thirty new suggestions. Tableaux, pantomimes, recitations, marches, drills, songs and special programs, provide exactly the right kind of material for Spring exercises of any sort. The drills and action pieces are fully illustrated. Everything in the book has been especially edited and arranged for it.

Select Speeches for Declamation
By John H. Bechtel

This book contains a large number of short prose pieces chosen from the leading writers and speakers of all ages and nations, and admirably adapted for use by college men. Only the very best, from a large store of choice material, was selected for this work. The names of Demosthenes, Livy, Kossuth, Bonaparte, Chatham, Burke, Macaulay, Hugo, Gladstone, Washington, Jefferson, Garfield, Harrison, Webster, Everett, Phillips, Curtis, Blaine, Beecher, Grady, Cleveland, McKinley, and Depew may serve to suggest the standard of the selections.

THE PENN PUBLISHING COMPANY
925-27 FILBERT STREET PHILADELPHIA

...perance Selections
By John H. Bechtel
For Readings and Recitations

...ns have been taken from the utterances of pulpit ...ne speeches of political leaders, and from the pens ...s. They depict the life of the drunkard, point out ...innings of vice, and illustrate the growth of the habit after another is sipped amid the pleasures and gayeties ...life. This volume appeals to human intelligence, and ...words of truth and wisdom that cannot be gainsaid.

Sunday-School Selections
By John H. Bechtel
For Readings and Recitations

This volume contains about 150 selections of unusual merit. Among them something will be found adapted to every occasion and condition where a choice reading or recitation may be wanted. Suitable provision has been made for the Church Social, the Sunday-school Concert, Teachers' Gatherings, Christian Endeavor Societies, Anniversary occasions, and every assemblage of a religious or spiritual character. Besides its value for readings and recitations, the pastor will find much in it to adorn his sermon, and the superintendent points by which to illustrate the Sunday-school lesson.

Sunday-School Entertainments

All new and original. The demand for a book of pleasing and appropriate Sunday-school entertainments is here supplied. The articles are largely in the nature of dialogues, tableaux, recitations, concert pieces, motion songs, dramatized Bible stories, and responsive exercises, all based upon or illustrating some Biblical truth. Special care has been taken to make provision for such occasions as Christmas, New Year's, Easter, Thanksgiving, and the full round of celebrations, so that no time or season is without a subject.

THE PENN PUBLISHING COMPANY
925-27 FILBERT STREET PHILADELPHIA

Money Making Entertainments

By Lizzie J. Rook *and* Mrs. E. J. H. Goodfellow

There is no better way to raise money for church, school, or benevolent purposes than by means of entertainments. This unique volume contains a great abundance of new and original material especially prepared for such occasions by two writers of wide experience in this line of work. In addition to the money making features there is also a large variety of entertainments and socials for home use.

Tableaux, Charades, *and* Pantomimes

This attractive volume is adapted alike to Parlor Entertainments, School and Church Exhibitions, and for use on the Amateur Stage. The department of Tableaux is unusually complete. Only such scenes as can be produced with the smallest number of auxiliaries have been selected. Tableaux, with readings from standard authors, form a very attractive feature, as do also the statuary scenes. The volume has recently been enlarged by the addition of a number of new and original charades, which add greatly to the attractiveness of the book.

School *and* Parlor Comedies

By B. L. C. Griffith

The dialogue is so spirited that the lines almost play themselves, so that the plays are sure to be acceptable even in the hands of only fairly competent performers. The situations are ingenious, and the plots are such as command the attention of an audience at the outset and hold it until the last line is given. The plays differ widely in character, thus affording an unusual variety. The scenery required in any instance is not difficult and may be easily arranged in the class room or in the private parlor.

THE PENN PUBLISHING COMPANY
925-27 FILBERT STREET PHILADELPHIA

Entertainment Books for Young People

Monologues *and* Novelties
By B. L. C. Griffith

In addition to the large number of new and original monologues in this book, it contains also a large collection of other features—such, for instance, as a Shadow Pantomime, a Chinese Wedding, a Recitation with Lesson Help, a Play, a Monologue in Pantomime, etc. The entertainments vary in length from five to twenty-five minutes, and are all of a high order of excellence. The book is brim full of the choicest and most artistic forms of entertainment.

Sketches, Skits and Stunts
By John T. McIntyre

Good vaudeville material, amateur or professional, is hard to get. This book contains an abundance of the best for both classes, all written to order by one who knows how to do it well. There are jokes, monologues, dialogues, stories, songs, sketches, parodies, short farces, and talking acts of the rapid-fire variety, all constructed for strictly laughing purposes.

How to Become a Public Speaker
By William Pittenger

This work shows in a simple and concise way how any person of ordinary perseverance and good common sense may become a ready and effective public speaker. He is here directed how to gather thoughts, how to arrange them to the best advantage, and how to form clear outlines. He is then told how to overcome timidity, how to secure ease and fluency of language, and how to acquire such a mastery of the arts of the orator as will give him confidence and power.

THE PENN PUBLISHING COMPANY

www.ingramcontent.com/pod-product-compliance
Lightning Source LLC
Chambersburg PA
CBHW020904230426
43666CB00008B/1311